Energy Ball

For

Peace Ceremony

Personal Health ~ Global Blessing

Jeffrey Goldstein

Printed in Israel

First Printing, 2018

Author Contact information:

jeffgoldstein89@gmail.com

Graphics & Cover Design: Ohad Kozlovski -

Ohad_koz@yahoo.com

Skech Artist: Roy Shinar -

www.royshinar.com

Disclaimer:

The Energy Ball is not a substitute for any medical advice: physically, psychologically or emotionally.

The information in this book is meant to complement and not replace advice given by a medical professional. Consult your appropriate medical practitioner and ask them if the Energy Ball is safe for you. Please be advised that the author, editors and publisher are not responsible for the results of the activities and ceremonies in this Book.

Energy Ball for Peace Ceremony
Personal Health ~ Global Blessing

Dedication

This guidebook is dedicated to **Creator, Angels, Planet Earth, and enthusiastic Light Workers**!

About the Writing

What an exciting and challenging adventure preparing and authoring this experiential manuscript. It has been a life transforming experience for me. To form an Energy Ball is simple, but to describe how to form one and use it to bring forth personal and global peaceful energy, has taken me on a fascinating, transforming and learning journey!

The information and activities in this book are from my personal experiences with the versatile Energy Ball. My goal is to help as many people as possible, live, think and act as energetically-aware human beings, and remember their Angelic qualities!

During the preparation of this manuscript, I am very thankful for the assistance of many wonderful Human Angels.

My wife, Leah, thank you for your constant encouragement, understanding heart, love, patience and insight into the material! Leah has made Energy Balls for years and, being a dancer, greatly assisted me with the dance activities.

I want to thank my team of writing coaches particularly, Belle Fine-Cohen, Sally Klein-Katz, Yocheved Abram and Marsea Spiegel for your guidance, encouragement and skill with the Energy Ball!

There were many others who helped and encouraged me: Robert and Gail Goldstein, Iris Sardas, Jeanne White Eagle, John Pehrson, Eliyahu Holley, Greg Goltsov, Judy and Norman Enteen, Dhyan Or, Joan Emmons, Ellen Kennedy, Rabbi Michael Klein-Katz, Yavin Klein-Katz, Lisa Talesnick, Jonathan Font Moxo, Zohar Gaon, Gina Ross, Rabbi Ruth and Michael Kagan, Ohad Kozlovski, Roy Shinar, Dola Caspi and many, many others. Thank you!!!

I would like to honor a few of the mystics, philosophers and teachers who have influenced me in my life's journey: Abraham, Father of the Jewish, Christian and Muslim people; Lloyd Meeker Sr. (Uranda); Martin Exeter; Lou Rotola; Omraam Mikhael Aivanhov; Peter Deunov; Black Elk, and many other Native American Medicine Men and Women; Richard Alpert; Alan Watts; Anastasia of the Ringing Cedar series; and many, many more amazing Human Angels!

Special Love and appreciation to: My sweet daughters, Lilach and Shira, for their joy of life, trust in me and love!

Forward

In a time of deep chaos and turmoil, when so many people worldwide are moving through a quagmire of emotional trauma, it takes strength to maintain a quiet centeredness, and great courage to continually come from love at all times. The truth is that there are few individuals on our planet who have this kind of focus and commitment. I have had the honor and privilege of knowing such a person, Jeff Goldstein.

I have known Jeff many years and have found him to be profound in his approach to life, and particularly to his circumstances inside one of the most pivotal places on earth: Jerusalem. His interaction with events inside Israel, as well as Palestine, has presented him with the perfect setting for what he calls Energy Balls. In the 1990s, when the situation in Israel and Palestine was being described as a Cold War, and tensions were accelerating, Jeff's determination to apply his spiritual wisdom inside the heated climate of the Middle East took an interesting turn. It was during this time that he found an avenue to help quell tensions and provide a space for healing at deep levels to take place for individuals, as well as for groups of people.

Jeff discovered that when he brought his hands together as though holding a ball, a powerful energy emanated, one that could be directed by intent and had the power to clear a space in a way that made communion without conflict possible. In other words, "…it is a simple way to clarify the atmosphere of a group, and provides a sound base for deeper discussion and interaction." This discovery and unique phenomenon Jeff describes in detail in his book, *Energy Ball for Peace Ceremony: Personal Health and Global Blessing.*

I have had personal experience with the Energy Ball process

and have seen the power of its effect. My hope is that Jeff's work will multiply and move with ease around our planet. Such gifts and visions are crucial to the survival and evolution of humankind, and to all life on our beloved earth.

Jeanne White Eagle ~ Author and Visionary
Co-Founder of the Interstellar Community Foundation
December, 2016

Prelude

"We have been all wrong! What we have called matter is energy, whose vibration has been lowered as to be perceptible to the senses." [Albert Einstein]

"Energy is everything – It is the essence of life!" [Ramana Pemmaraju]

Everything is energy. Everything we perceive to exist is vibrating in a dynamic but unseen dance of molecules, atoms and subatomic particles. Even what we consider to be solid matter is mostly space. In fact, physicists tell us that the atoms that make up matter turn out to be 99.9999% space. This means that what we see as solid matter isn't really solid. The perception is more like an agreement that humans make to perceive our physical surroundings as real.

Einstein, one of the smartest persons ever to have lived, showed the convertibility of energy and matter in his now famous equation, $E = mc2$. Matter is really condensed energy whose vibration has slowed down enough so we can see it.

The point is this: energy is the essence of everything, and everything is energy. What Jeff Goldstein calls the magical natural world is everywhere filled with energy that is ready to be harnessed, if you know how.

In his book, Jeff Goldstein shows us how to harness the energy of our own bodies and the natural world, and direct this energy back into the world of human existence for a variety of positive, healing and uplifting purposes, many of which are described in simple, straightforward terms in the following pages.

If you are just learning about energy and energy healing, this manual will transform your life. You will learn to tap into the energy that is all around you, and direct its healing power inward to yourself and outward to others, individually or collectively. As you begin to experience the healing benefits personally, and see outcomes shift around you, it will alter forever how you see and interact with the world. You will begin to realize that everything is alive in its subtle yet unseen dance of energy and vibration. You will also realize that everything is connected to everything else, a realization that will engender deep respect for the natural world and deep compassion for others.

If you are already familiar with energy and energy healing, this book will teach you another simple and straightforward method for working with and channeling energy in various ways to help yourself and others, and to leave the planet in a little better shape than it is currently. Practicing Jeff Goldstein's Energy Ball technique will restore or renew your faith in energy work, and add another tool to your toolbox, another arrow in the quiver, so to speak.

I can see a time when many people will know how to form Energy Balls, and use them to create radiant health and peace on the planet. As the world seems to be deeply mired in chaos and conflict as I write this, this goal may seem out of reach. But just think of the potential of thousands of people working with energy to create a better world. If this were so, together we could create irrevocable and lasting good in the world.

It remains to say that my wife, Jeanne White Eagle, and I have known Jeff Goldstein for many years now. We have participated in some of his ceremonies and peace events in Israel, and they have always been powerful. I have rarely met a person who walks his talk so consistently and with such unobtrusive passion. He lives in integrity, by which I mean to say that his inner and outer life, his personal and public life are all in alignment, something that is quite rare.

The process that he describes in his book is easy to learn and powerful to work with. Over time, with practice, it could transform your life and, ultimately, the world!

John B. Pehrson: Author of Mystical Numerology:
The Creative Power of Sounds and Numbers
December, 2016

Table of Contents

Section 1
Beginning

Overview

"Energy cannot be created or destroyed, it can only be changed from one form to another." Albert Einstein

This guidebook is about the Energy Ball. The Energy Ball is formed between your hands and provides simple access to connect to and influence the flow of Life Energy moving through your physical body.

With a little information, you can charge Life Energy with nourishing, peaceful vibrations and change yourself and your environment.

Terms

The following terms are used throughout the guidebook:

- **Energy** ~ universal current of life.
- **Energy Ball** ~ formed by containing Life Energy between the hands.
- **Peace** ~ natural, calming vibration that transforms chaos into stillness.
- **Ceremony** ~ specific time to consciously focus Life Energy.
- **Collective Energy Ball for Peace Ceremony** ~ a group that utilizes the collective current of life to create an atmosphere for peace.
- **Personal Health** ~ enlivening the body's cells with Life Energy, promoting an atmosphere for self-healing, and developing the ability to live radiantly on Planet Earth.
- **Global Blessing** ~ radiant human beings coming together as a team to create an atmosphere of peace, thereby nurturing and blessing humanity.

Guidebook structure

This guidebook is divided into sections, all of which contain one or more chapters. The sections are structured as follows:

- **Section 1** welcomes and introduces you to the guidebook.
- **Section 2** shows you how to form the Energy Ball and ways to use it to care for yourself. It includes different Energy Ball hand positions, which expand its usage.
- **Section 3** takes you through the phases of the Collective Energy Ball for Peace Ceremony, and provides a script for you to conduct the Ceremony. This explanation is followed by enjoyable and inspiring Collective activities that bless the world!
- **Section 4** takes you deeper into understanding the Energy Ball and the consciousness surrounding it.
- **Section 5** assists you in incorporating the Energy Ball into your daily life.
- **Chapter 18** enables you to share and spread peaceful vibrations with your Energy Ball.

Enjoy your journey into the world of Energy!!

Chapter 1
Welcome to the Energy Ball
for Peace Ceremony!!

- Introduction
- History of the Energy Ball for Peace Ceremony
- About the Energy Ball
- The Energy Ball for Peace Ceremony
- Learning Suggestions
- Learning Goals
- Story ~ Jerusalem Celebration of Light!

Introduction

As a young child, I realized that a magical world exists known as the natural world. I also realized that we live on a planet that does not respect the natural world, and this disrespect results in complicated problems.

I chose to explore the magical natural world and discovered unique ways to bring nature's pure vibration into my personal life. This led me in fascinating directions, and brought me great amounts of insight and pleasure.

Looking at the rest of humanity, I saw a different picture: disrespect was rampant! With a deep yearning to help, I began to think all the time, of ways to bring nature's magic into the lives of other human beings.

As part of my spiritual search, in the early 1970's I was

introduced to Life Energy and the Energy Ball, in an energetic therapy called Attunement[1]. Immediately, I realized that what was between my hands was something powerful and life changing! It thrilled me, and I began to explore and explore and explore!

Now I had the Energy Ball and Attunement as energetic tools for my and other people's personal growth and self–alignment! Wow, my life began to change, with the invisible world becoming tangible!

In the early 1990's, after returning to Jerusalem, I started to combine the Energy Ball with my passion for spiritual peace. I found the Energy Ball to be a simple way to clarify the atmosphere of a group, and provide a sound basis for deeper discussion and interaction.

Since that time, I have shared the Energy Ball with many individuals and spiritual peace groups in Israel, Palestine, Europe, and America. This led to the development of the Energy Ball for Peace Ceremony, and the writing of this guidebook. Enjoy your adventure with it, I certainly have enjoyed writing these words for you!!

History of the Energy Ball for Peace Ceremony

After moving to Jerusalem in the 1990's, I began to attend peace gatherings. Shortly, I learned that there are hundreds of peace groups in Israel and Palestine, each with a different purpose and goal. I decided to focus my attention on the spiritual peace groups that promote the consciousness of peace. During these gatherings, life's stories are shared, and the atmosphere of friendly neighbors is built. A wide variety of activities are used, including conflict resolution training, talking circles, music, art,

---

1 See Attunement, page 207.

dance, sports, nature, adventure, and drinking tea and coffee while sitting around the campfire!

After I participated for a while, I realized that there was a genuine need for groups of peace people to come together and have meaningful experiences. Knowing that the Energy Ball brings on a peaceful atmosphere, I began to show individuals and groups how to form the Energy Ball and merge together as a team. This grew into what I called Energy Circles.

This spread into several directions:

- Creating and coordinating the **Jerusalem Celebration of Light Gathering** in the Jerusalem forest once a year, for 12 years. There were many Energy Ball for Peace Ceremonies during this festive event![2]

- **Guiding and teaching** individuals to utilize the Energy Ball for personal healing and helping other people.

- **Healing and Dance** ~ a weekly event my wife, Leah, and I created, where people learned to dance with the Energy Ball. It developed into seminars called Heartdance. Leah became a DJ, and I began to teach classes and offer couple blending ceremonies with the Energy Ball.

- **Sunday Middle East Peace Blessing Ceremony** ~ weekly, long-distance Energy Ball event that has been sending its blessing to Jerusalem and the Middle East since the late 1990's. Peace people from all around the globe participate every Sunday evening (21:00- 21:30 IST).

- **Conducting over a thousand** Energy Ball for Peace Ceremonies in Israel and Palestine. A few examples:
  - **All Nations Café** ~ This mobile café is made up of good-hearted people from Israel and Palestine. In

---

2   See Jerusalem Celebration of Light Gathering, page 11

recent years, we meet near the spring, Ein Haniya, in Al-Walaja, a Palestinian village between Bethlehem and Jerusalem. We sit around the fire, drink tea and coffee, eat, tell stories about our lives, and experience the atmosphere of peace together. The Energy Ball for Peace Ceremony provides a wonderful opportunity to learn from one another and bond together as friends.

- **Jerusalem Peace Circles** ~ For over two years, a group of spiritual peace activists met weekly in a circular sitting area in a park off Bezalel Street, in downtown Jerusalem. We promoted the consciousness of peace through singing, sharing circles and the Energy Ball for Peace Ceremony. We met a wide variety of wonderful people, from the community, and being Jerusalem, around the world. It was a transforming experience for all! (During the editing a friend called and wants to restart this group in the same location!)

- **Peace Circle at the Boogie** ~ The Boogie is Jerusalem's "free dance", that has been happening under various names since 1980's. At the beginning of the evening the Energy Ball sparks dancing energy; and at closure, it brings dancers into a meditative dance space, always amazing, fun and dynamic!

- **Sulha Peace Project** ~ The Sulha is a peace initiative that gathers Israeli and Palestinian peace activists together to meet one another, become friends, and share about what it is like to live on the other side. The Energy Ball for Peace Ceremonies assist in stimulating inner peace from the participants, give us the opportunity to meet one another, and assist to send forth collective Peace Blessings.

As time went on, the tool of the Energy Circle grew, so we added a word in front such as: Peace Energy Circles, Healing Energy Circles, Dancing Energy Circles and eventually, Energy Ball for Peace Ceremony.

Personally, I am very thankful that the Energy Ball for Peace Ceremony has helped turn many regular humans into Peace People!

About the Energy Ball

The Energy Ball is formed by containing Life Energy between the hands[3]. They are held close to each other, thereby compacting the Life Energy coming out of them. After a few moments, the intensity of Life Energy builds up, and it can be felt in the hands as sensations[4].

When Life Energy comes out of the hands on a consistent basis, the Energy Ball becomes natural and a powerful life tool!

The Energy Ball affects each person in a unique way, and its ability to help varies according to the setting and the amount of people participating. The Energy Ball has great possibilities to assist with personal health, growth and development[5].

When the Energy Ball combines with intention, it creates blessings, health, and peaceful vibrations.

The Energy Ball for Peace Ceremony

After conducting Energy Circles for years, I realized that I was actually leading a ceremony.

The ceremony can be experienced individually and in a group.

---

3   See Creating the Energy Ball, page 16
4   See What Happens when an Energy Ball is Formed? page 32
5   Appendix 2, page 208

The purpose being, to amplify the vibration of spiritual peace and spread blessings.

The phases of the Ceremony are:

- Preparation ~ entering ceremony time with gentle, peaceful thoughts.
- Creation of an Energy Ball ~ circulating compacted Life Energy between the hands.
- Merging two or more Energy Balls together ~ creating a unified and intensified collective Energy Ball.
- Blessing the Energy Ball ~ encoding the Energy Ball with sacred words, welcoming Creator and Angelic friends to participate in sending blessings of peace.
- Releasing the Energy Ball ~ lifting the Energy Ball upwards and spreading the peaceful vibration.

There are various techniques to enrich the Energy Ball, giving it versatility! They are found in chapters 4 and 15.

Learning Suggestions

These ideas assist you to deepen your experience with the guidebook:

- Form Energy Balls often during the reading. This will make it so that the Energy Ball becomes natural to you and part of your life.
- Do the Hand Positions Practice several times to learn each position's name[6].
- When you hold an Energy Ball, notice how the Life Energy flows through your body, and how it affects your emotions and your thoughts.

---

6   *See Hand Positions Practice, page 36*

- Pay attention to how the Energy Ball stimulates your spirit and the invisible world around you.

- Become familiar with the unique way in which I use words[7].

- Take your time during reading, and practice the activities. This will deepen your body wisdom.

- Become skillful with the Energy Ball by intuitively sensing which activities are correct for you each day.

- Be attentive to the words you use, and the tone of your voice while giving blessings.

- Develop a solid connection between your spirit, body, emotions and mental capacity, by respecting and nurturing each of them with the assistance of the Energy Ball.

- Rinse your hands in water before and after the Energy Ball exercises, to experience Life Energy with more

- precision and clarity.

- If you already know how to form an Energy Ball, use the Enrichment Techniques to make it more versatile[8].

If you wish to be a leader of the Collective Energy Ball for Peace Ceremony, two readings of this book are recommended: one from a personal view, and the other from the viewpoint of a leader.

Learning Goals

This guidebook instructs you how to:

- Use the Energy Ball daily to improve your life quality!

- Live in attunement with your life essence

---

7   See Nuances, page 122
8   See Enrichment Techniques, page 36

- Increase clarity in your spirituality
- Feel an increased energy flow in your body
- View the environment with more awareness of its natural sacred beautiful energy
- Bring the spirit of peace into our world!

Story ~ Jerusalem Celebration of Light!

I was honored to be the coordinator of the Jerusalem Celebration of Light Gathering for 12 years! What an adventure we had each year at this two-day festival. Many hundreds of radiant, beautiful, wonderful people attended.

The purpose of our gathering was to send a collective burst of light and peace to Jerusalem and all of creation. The Energy Ball for Peace Ceremony was the way we focused and sent out our blessings.

The gathering took place in the Jerusalem Forest on a hilltop called Mitzpeh Kerem (Hirbet Hamame). It is located just behind the Holocaust Memorial, The Valley of the Communities, at Yad Vashem.

Mitzpeh Kerem is not just any hilltop. It is an Earth Energy Vortex. This means that this part of Planet Earth sends out an extra strong and unique vibration of earth energy. It has two parts:

- A solid natural rock semicircle, with an opening in the center, that I call "Grandmother Circle".
- A unique rock formation and stone cove on the peak of the hill, where there is a near panoramic view of Jerusalem and the surrounding hills.

During the gathering, we utilized the strong earth energy coming out of this hill, combined with the Energy Ball for Peace Ceremony to help intensify our radiant light into the world.

How It Started:

After coming to Jerusalem in 1993, I met a continuous flow of people who, like myself, had a deep passion for peace. I named us "Peace People".

We met many times to discuss how our group could bring a greater amount of light into our world, and stimulate the spirit of peace in Jerusalem. During these meetings, we realized that communication and respect are the keys to creating peaceful relationships with our neighbors.

After consideration, we came up with the idea of having a two-day light gathering in Jerusalem on the full moon in the spring. We invited everyone we knew to join us. Peace people from Israel, Palestine, and around the world attended. Rather than charge a fee, we asked participants to make a financial love offering to help cover our expenses.

In preparation, we created a schedule of events. Someone volunteered to be in charge of the kitchen, another person made signs, and we considered everything we needed for a gathering of about 100 people. We decided when and where to have the Energy Ball for Peace Ceremonies and other activities.

The first day of the gathering we were really happy as we watched a constant flow of excited Peace People arrive on the hilltop. Many more than the 100 people we expected attended! This gathering turned into a festival of light – vibrant, radiant!

During the 12 years, each gathering built upon the previous year's gathering. This developed a very refined quality of light in the peace people who attended and created a very strong peace team. Each year, the attendance varied between 300 and 1,500 peace people.

During Jerusalem Celebration of Light, I led many Energy Ball for Peace Ceremonies.

The first ceremony was Friday midday:

- It brought together helper energy, honoring those who had spent time preparing for the gathering.
- It was a time to bless those who were traveling to Mitzpeh Kerem (Hirbet Hamame) and the gathering.
- It initiated Grandmother Circle as a Sacred Space, and the central location for all the participants to assemble.

At Sunset, the entire group came together at Grandmother Circle for a Collective Energy Ball for Peace Ceremony, which led into a singing Kabbalat Shabbat (welcoming in of the Sabbath). It was a festive bringing in of the Shekinah (the Sabbath Bride) and the spirit of peace! We sang, danced, prayed, and sent out a large burst of light energy to Jerusalem and the world.

At midnight on the top of the hill of Mitzpeh Kerem, the Energy Ball for Peace Ceremony guided us into a deep meditation, and connected us with the Mystical Earth Energy Vortex.

The ceremony on Shabbat (Saturday) morning brought together the intention of the day. We prepared the energy of the camp for the upcoming activities, and welcomed in a fresh burst of exciting energy from new participants!

The midday Energy Ball for Peace Ceremony was usually the largest circle during the Jerusalem Celebration of Light Gathering. It included peace prayers and blessings, in many languages, from religious and community leaders. We focused on lifting up our light and sharing it with Jerusalem to bring the spirit of peace to the city and all of its residents.

The Jerusalem Celebration of Light Gathering officially ended at Sunset with a closing Energy Ball for Peace Ceremony, where participants shared their experiences and prepared for the next year's gathering.

Our final Energy Ball for Peace Ceremony was Sunday morning with those who remained overnight, and the cleanup crew. It was a special opportunity to review the festival and honor the helpers.

Many other activities occurred at the gathering:

There were activities and workshops, including Attunement, Reiki, meditation, drawing, Hebrew letter movements, maze walk, nature adventures, dance classes, darbuka lessons, drum circles, singing circles, and other energizing activities. In the evening, participants gathered around small campsite fires singing songs, and philosophizing about how to create a peaceful society.

We had many Peaceful Guests including: Sufis, Tibetan monks, African shamans, priests, sisters, sheikhs, rabbis, Native American elders and many everyday people who simply loved shining their light!

One year, The World Peace Prayer Society donated a peace pole with the statement *May Peace Prevail on Earth* inscribed on it in four languages[9].

Another year, a Native American peace pipe ceremony was conducted, plus many more peace creating ceremonies and activities[10].

I was the coordinator of the Jerusalem Celebration of Light gathering for 12 years. It was an amazing and transformative experience. I learned about people, peace, healing, and how powerful the Energy Ball for Peace Ceremony actually is! It was wonderful to witness those who attended being transformed into radiant human beings – Peace People!

It has been many years since the last gathering, and I still run into people asking me to organize another gathering.

Maybe one day.............

---

9   *See Peace Pole, page 198*
10 *Story ~ Jeanne White Eagle and John Pehrson page 204*

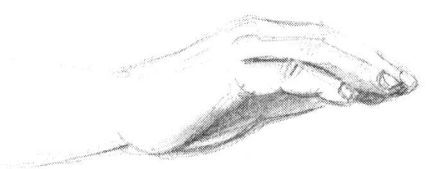

Section 2
Personal Ceremony

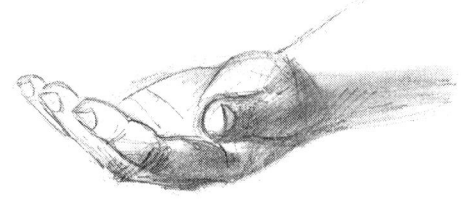

Chapter 2: Creating the Energy Ball

These are the steps needed to form an Energy Ball, and some beginning practices:

- Preparation
- Connecting to Your Hands
- Perceiving the Energy
- Forming the Ball
- Allowing and Noticing
- Blessings and the Energy Ball
- Spreading the Energy Ball
- Waterfall of Liquid Light
- Visualizing the Energy Ball
- Opening Hand Sensations
- Story ~ Energy Ball with Etheric Hands

Preparation

To create the best conditions in which to form an Energy Ball:

- Find a quiet location for your ceremony, a place where you will not be disturbed.
- Turn off cell phones and put them and any metal objects into your bag, including watches, jewelry (except wedding rings), keys, cell phones, etc.
- Give your hands a fresh start, by washing them in water. If water is not available, then cleanse your hands by visualizing water pouring over them.
- Place your current thoughts on the side of your consciousness, giving yourself space to be perceptive and sense the Energy coming out of your hands.

• Turn your consciousness to peaceful thoughts!

Connecting to Your Hands

Hands are amazing, we use them in so many unique and specific ways. The following activity brings awareness to your hands and assists them to sense the flow of Life Energy. For those who do not have use of their hands, use your imagination.[11] Look at your hands with a steady focus.

• Consider the unique ways that we utilize our hands: dressing, eating, steering cars, writing, playing instruments, typing, creating, comforting, helping others, to name just a few.

• Be grateful for their usage by remembering some of their recent activities and how they served you.

• Move your hands around exploring their flexibility.

• Stretch the fingers as wide as you can; then relax them.

• Shake your hands, noticing the tingling sensation from having an increased supply of blood.

• Massage your hands, this loosens and stimulates the muscles and abundant nerve endings in the fingers and palms.

• Appreciate the power of your hands, honoring and preparing them for clearer perception.

Perceiving the Energy

To stimulate the perceiving part of your hands, do the following:

With your fingers and palms held straight, bring your hands very close together, almost touching. Pay attention to what you sense between your hands. This is the Perceiving position.

---

11   See *Energy Ball with Etheric Hands, page 25*

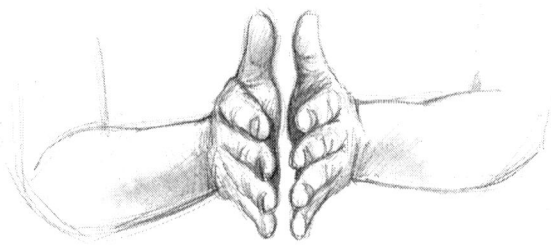

You may experience many sensations:

- Flowing sensation ~ awareness of the movement of Life Energy.
- Tingling sensation ~ the hands are waking up to subtle energy vibrations
- Movement ~ the hands are pushed back and forth creating a magnetic vibration.
- Heat ~ a warm to very hot sensation. This is evidence that the flow of Life Energy in the hands is increasing. Some people's hands can sweat from the Life Energy moving through them!

Forming the Ball

1. From the Perceiving position, slightly bend your fingers creating a circular space between your hands. This is the space where Life Energy concentrates and circulates.

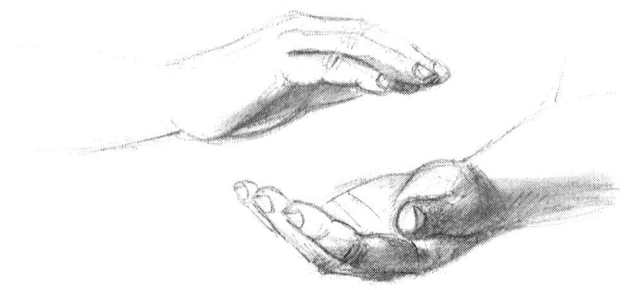

2. Notice that you just created an Energy Ball!

3. Keep your hands close together, this allows you to become acquainted with the sensation and to perceive the compacted Life Energy flow.

4. Pay attention to how the sensation between your hands changes.

5. Notice your breathing, and how the awareness of your breath affects the Energy Ball.

6. If the sensation vanishes, start again in the Perceiving Position and then form the Energy Ball, or you can ask someone who feels the Energy Ball to help you, using the *Opening Hand Sensations* activity[12].

Allowing and Noticing

Allowing builds patience and noticing builds confidence!

Now that you have made the Energy Ball, allow it to build its intensity by collecting and organizing your body's vibrations. This usually takes a few minutes, during this time, notice the many nuances of the Energy Ball and how you relate to the vibrations in it. Closing your eyes helps.

Noticing acquaints you with the Energy Ball's changing sensations. As you recognize these sensations, their meaning opens up to you. This is the *Language of Light Energy.*[13]

Blessings and the Energy Ball

Blessings encode the Energy Ball with intention and welcome Creator and Angels[14] to participate. There are Self-Blessings

---

12 *See Opening Hand Sensations, page 23*
13 *See Language of Light Energy, page 130*
14 *See Creator and Angelic Friends, page 137*

which assist in the connection between the physical and spiritual realities, and there are Radiant Blessings that guide the healing light to a person, place or situation.

During the Peace Ceremony, after Life Energy is focused in the hands, words are spoken that carry the intended purpose of the ceremony. The words are complemented by the tone of the voice and the person's quality of spirit.

Many of the activities have suggested Blessings, you can use them and create your own by using these ingredients:

- A deep gratitude, appreciation and love for Creator and your Angelic Friends.
- An awesome respect for the natural cycles and process of life.
- An acknowledgement that it is sacred to be alive and to breathe the breath of life!

Spreading the Energy Ball

After you have encoded the Energy Ball with your Blessing, raise it up very slowly into the Earth's atmosphere. This releases the Energetic Blessing, and with the assistance of your Angelic Friends, the Encoded Energy Ball is guided with its sacred Blessings and Healing Power as a gift to all of creation!

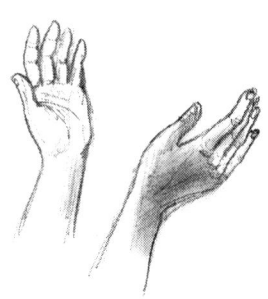

Cleansing the Hands

After you have released the Energy Ball and before you form another Energy Ball, refresh and restart your hands by cleansing them.

Water is best, it easily neutralizes energetic vibrations, increases your hands' perceptive abilities and gives them a fresh start.

When water is unavailable, use the following *Waterfall of Liquid Light activity.*

Waterfall of Liquid Light

This activity increases the flow of light energy through your body, neutralizes impure energy and refreshes your overall energy body![15]

1. Hold your hands facing upwards at waist height in the Cleansing position.

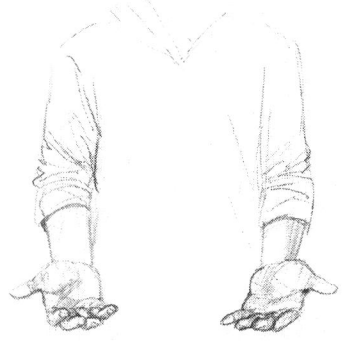

---

15 *See Impure Energy, page 123*

2. Visualize yourself under a waterfall or your shower at home.

3. Imagine the water as liquid light energy flowing around your body, cleansing and washing away heavy, needy, sticky vibrations!

4. Then invite light energy to enter into your body cleansing and nourishing your cells.

5. Focus your attention on the light energy flowing through the systems of your body. Envisioning this liquid light entering into your nerves and releasing any limiting vibrations.

6. Notice how active and happy your cells become when they are cleansed and nourished by the liquid light!!

7. Stay in this infinite liquid light for as long as you wish, allowing it to refresh you and melt away old worries and feelings at the same time.

8. Notice that your overall energy body feels lighter, and that there is a tickling sensation inside your body.

9. Rub your body gently for a few moments, then rinse your hands in water.

Remember what it feels like to be Blessed and cleansed inside and around your body!

Repeat this activity whenever you wish to feel purer and clearer!

Visualizing the Energy Ball

It is an integrative experience to form an Energy Ball and imagine one at the same time.

1. Form the Energy Ball in the Charging position.

2. Look at your hands and pay attention to their colors, texture, and shape.

3. Use your peripheral vision and bring your attention to the space between your hands; noticing the puffy dots and waves of energy[16].

4. Remember how the Energy Ball looks by taking a memory snapshot. This is done by imagining that your thoughts are like the memory card in a camera and you blink your eyes to take the picture.

5. After a short time, open your eyes and once again look at and into the Energy Ball. Notice how it has changed and become more etheric! Take another memory snapshot and once again close your eyes and visualize it.

6. Go back and forth between gazing into and visualizing the Energy Ball. Going at a steady pace allows you to experience them as one.

This exercise assists you to form an Energy Ball anytime you wish. It works wonderfully!!

Opening Hand Sensations

There can be many reasons why a person cannot sense the Energy flow between their hands[17].

To help someone who does not feel the Energy Ball, assist them with the following activity:

1. Ask them to massage their hands and explain to them this loosens their muscles.

2. Have them shake their hands so that they stimulate the nerve endings in the fingers and palms.

3. Ask them to hold their hands a few centimeters apart in the Perceiving position.

---

16   *See Spiritual Sight Development, page 163*
17   *See Not Feeling the Energy Ball? on page 30*

4. Then place your hands around their hands without touching them.

5. Look into their eyes and make a spiritual connection.

6. Have them pay attention to their breathing.

7. Ask them what they sense between their hands. Give them examples, such as warmth, magnetic pulsing, or a tingling sensation.

8. When they sense the energy flow, continue to hold your hands around theirs, enabling their sensation of the Energy Ball to intensify.

9. After a minute, ask them to bend their fingers and form the Energy Ball and notice what they sense.

10. Slowly take your hands away from theirs until they are holding the Energy Ball on their own.

11. If they still do not sense the energy, place your hand slightly above one of their forearms and ask them if they feel anything. Invite them to do the same to your forearm and tell you what sensations they feel. Then go back to the Perceiving position and form the Energy Ball.

Story ~ Energy Ball with Etheric Hands

A close friend of mine, Eliyahu Holley, was a quadriplegic. In the 1990's he was my Attunement student. Since he was unable to use his physical hands, he imagined forming the Energy Ball with his Etheric Hands. To share an Attunement, he would visualize the Energy Ball and with his intent, send Life Energy to his nervous system and endocrine glands. This helped him to feel stronger, assist other people and develop his Spiritual Sight.

He was quite an amazing human being, happy and ready to help others! He hosted many spiritual events at his home near Jerusalem and created a YouTube video series[18], interviewing many amazing people.

During my review of this book, I visited Eliyahu and read him some parts of the manuscript, asking for his thoughts. About a week later he called me and said that he has been waking up in the middle of the night and becoming bored. He wanted to do something, but he did not want to wake his wife or caretakers, and unfortunately, he could not get his book to read on his own. Then he remembered the Energy Ball, imagined it, and began to stare into it. This took him into a deep, deep mystical meditation! The Energy Ball became a doorway for him to his higher consciousness in October 2017.

On November 16, 2017, Eliyahu turned into an etheric Angel, when his body passed away; leaving two radiant children and his amazing wife, Leehee.

---

18   See Eliyahu Holley's YouTube video:
https://www.youtube.com/user/ElijahsCodes

Chapter 3
Information and Questions

In this chapter, there is information that will help you to utilize the Energy Ball.

- Hand Positions
- Hand Movement Meanings
- Not Feeling the Energy Ball?
- How Long to Hold the Energy Ball?
- Can you Cause Harm with the Energy Ball?
- What Happens When you Form an Energy Ball?
- The Ah Ha! Experience
- Religion and the Energy Ball
- Children and the Energy Ball

Hand Positions

The Energy Ball is used in different hand positions for various purposes. Here are a few and how they are used:

1. **Perceiving position** ~ Hold your hands as close as possible to each other without touching, fingers and palms held straight. This position brings awareness to hand sensations.

2. **Nurturing position** ~ Hold one hand vertically above the other, either hand on top. This position contains and guides Life Energy into your body. You can use it to activate self-healing and build inner strength.

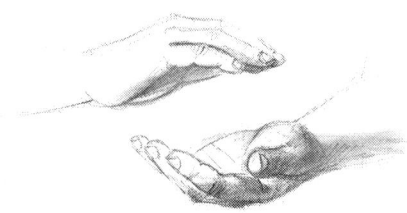

3. **Charging position** ~ Position your hands horizontally facing each other. This position contains Life Energy and builds its density. It creates a defined area to encode the Energy Ball with Blessing.

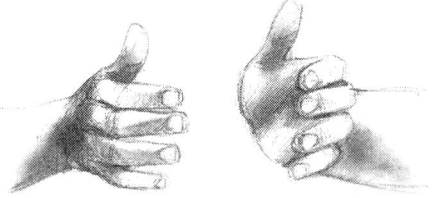

4. **Radiant position** ~ Hold your hands with your palms facing away from the body. The Energy Ball turns into a stream of Life Energy coming out of your hands. You can use this stream to spread Blessings. You can also use this position to sense energetic vibrations from afar. There are two positions:

- **The upper position**, where you hold your hands at chest height

- **The lower position**, where you hold your hands by your thighs.

5. **Light Connection position** ~ With palms facing upwards, extend both of your arms towards the sky, with your feet planted solidly on the ground, connected to Planet Earth. Creator's eternal flow of light energy enters your hands, travels through your entire body, and enters into and feeds Planet Earth. This turns your body into a channel of light! This position connects Creator to the Planet Earth, welcomes in Angelic Friends, and creates a space for transformation.

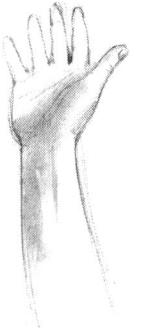 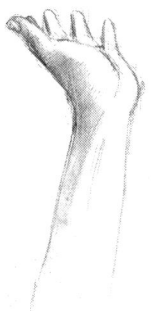

6. **Grounding position** ~ Hold your hands with your palms facing downward. This position sends Life Energy into the ground and connects to Planet Earth. There are two positions:

- **The upper position**, where you hold your hands at waist height

- **The lower position**, where you hold your hands close to the ground.

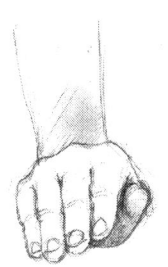 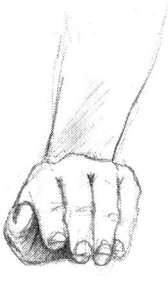

7. **Cleansing position** ~ Hold your palms facing upwards at waist height. Life Energy enters your hands, and purifies your body's energy flow.

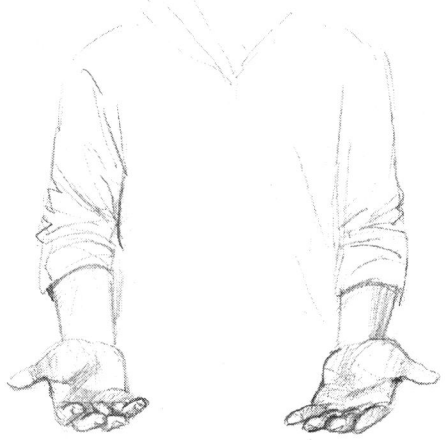

To practice these hand positions, see the reference Hand Positions Practice[19].

Hand Movement Meanings

When the hands move on their own while forming an Energy Ball, it means the following to me:

• Hands move outwards ~ the Life Energy is filling up the space and wishes to expand.

---

19 *See Hand Positions Practice, page 36.*

- Hands move inwards ~ the Life Energy is condensing and entering into the body.
- Hands move keep moving ~ the Life Energy is organizing.

Understanding vibrations in the Energy Ball helps to learn the language of light energy.

Not Feeling the Energy Ball?

Life Energy constantly flows through the body, so why is it more difficult for some people to feel the Energy Ball?

There are many reasons:

- Not recognizing the sensation in the hands as the flow of Life Energy
- Inexperience: not being trained to feel Life Energy
- Consciously preoccupied, and not currently available to experience such sensations
- Unclear past experiences with feeling energy
- Disconnection from the body's Life Energy flow

The degree to which Life Energy is felt in the hands depends upon how well the person is connected to their body sensations.

How Long to Hold the Energy Ball?

The Energy Ball has many purposes, each circumstance requires a different length of time.

- For relaxation, you can hold it for 5-10 minutes.
- For a quick discharge of your nervous system, hold it for 30 seconds to 2 minutes.
- For sleeping and to reach a deep meditative state, hold the Energy Ball until you are no longer aware that you are holding it.

- To work through a problem, hold the Energy Ball until your emotions and nervous system calm down. This will provide you time and energy to more effectively deal with the situation.

- For emergency - situations, handle the emergency first; afterwards, calm down with the Energy Ball.

- For fun and enjoyment, you can hold the Energy Ball as long as you wish. Listen to the Energy Ball, it will guide you.

Can You Cause Harm with the Energy Ball?

Some people are concerned about harming others with the Energy Ball.

As long as you have the consciousness and attitude of giving, respect, and unconditional love, Life Energy is charged with the sacred, and cannot cause harm. Rather, it stimulates the Life Energy flow.

When a person is disrespectful, hateful, and has a getting, needy attitude, they create an atmosphere around them that causes harm.

I am not experienced with forming the Energy Ball with a disrespectful attitude, so I have no idea what would actually happen. However, the following is what I believe would probably occur to the person:

- The sensation of feeling Life Energy in their hands would diminish.

- Their body's Life Energy flow would turn into a sticky substance, clogging the internal pathways.

- They would become exhausted and lose their vitality.

- Their body tissues would no longer receive healthy Life

Energy, resulting in internal sadness and an atmosphere conducive to for developing disease.

- Their thought processes would become sluggish and unrealistic, and they would cause harm with their words and actions.

What Happens when you form an Energy Ball?

The following conclusions are not scientifically proven, but are based on my own personal experiences:

- Life Energy circulates through the nerves of the hands and intensifies the circulation of life in the entire body.

- After a short time, surface tension in the central nervous system begins to discharge and the breath becomes quieter.

- Then the hormones receive the signal, rest period, and begin to calm down.

- An autonomic breath happens, discharging the autonomic nervous system.

- The conscious mind becomes less active as it observes.

- The emotions open up to inner sensations and moment by moment body experiences.

- The body-spirit connection strengthens, and insights are received.

This does not take place each time an Energy Ball is made. With experience, the deeper experiences with the Energy Ball take place.

The Ah Ha! Experience

"Wow! This is the real thing! It is an actual experience!" I have often heard this reaction, when someone feels Energy flowing through their hands for the first time.

Feeling the energy in the hands creates a confirmation and validation that Life Energy exists, and it builds confidence. "Yes, there is something happening in and around my body. The invisible world is real. Ah ha!"

As you continue to form Energy Balls, many more *Ah Ha!* experiences will come to you......

Religion and the Energy Ball

I have conducted many Energy Ball for Peace Ceremonies with people from all the major religions. The responses I receive are that the Energy Ball is acceptable according to their religious beliefs.

Because the Energy Ball for Peace Ceremony is a non-touch event, most religions have no restrictions about it.

Some religions have rules about how close a person can be to the other gender. Therefore, the person should stand next to others of the same gender.

Religious Blessings are welcome during the Energy Ball for Peace Ceremony. They can be said silently, or coordinated with the leader of the ceremony.

Children and the Energy Ball

Children inherently know and sense Life Energy. Usually, the Energy Ball feels very natural to them, and they enjoy the experience. Once a child learns the Energy Ball, they are able to form one quite easily.

To teach children the Energy Ball:

- Form Energy Balls in their presence, and provide them with the opportunity to become acquainted and intrigued by Life Energy.

- Explain to them that the Energy Ball is a non-touch experience, and it may seem a little strange at first, but soon it will become natural to them.

- Children like to have a choice. It does not work to impose the Energy Ball upon them.

- Children react to feeling Life Energy slightly differently than an adult. Ask them what they sense.

- Just because a child has smaller size hands, this does not mean that the energy coming out of these small hands is less powerful.

- When a child begins to utilize the Energy Ball early in life, they develop more naturally, healthier, and with richer experiences.

- Children of all ages are welcome in the Collective Energy Ball for Peace Ceremony when accompanied by a responsible adult.

- If you are not the guardian of the child, ask for parental permission.

I suggest the following way to introduce the Energy Ball to a child:

1. I just learned about the Energy Ball and it really helps me to calm down and focus myself, and it is fun! Would you like to form one with me?

2. If they wish to know more, explain to them that Life Energy constantly and abundantly flows through the body. It is possible to contain and compact Life Energy with the hands and form an Energy Ball.

3. Invite them to place one of their hands close to your Energy Ball and ask them if they can feel something.

4. Let them interact with the Energy Ball in any way that they wish, even make it into a fun game.

5. Teach them the Perceiving position and how to form the Energy Ball, by using the information in Section 2.[20]

---

20 *See Section 2, page 15.*

Chapter 4: Enrichment Techniques

This chapter contains the following practice exercises that assist you to influence and utilize Life Energy between your hands.

- Hand Position Practice
- Hand Massage
- Pumping the Energy Ball
- Encoding the Energy Ball
- Blowing into the Energy Ball
- Filling up the Energy Ball
- Stimulating the Fingers
- Smiling with the Energy Ball
- Energy Ball Using your Feet

Hand Position Practice

This activity helps you learn and practice the main Energy Ball positions used in this guidebook.

1. Start with the Perceiving position, and sense what is taking place in and around your body.

2. Move your hands into the Nurturing position, and allow Life Energy to enter inside of your body and fill it up with light.

3. Move into the Charging position. Allow the Energy Ball to fill up, and then expand it around your body.

4. Move into the Radiant position. Send your Blessing outwards, and receive information.

5. Move into the Light Connection position. Experience being in a channel of light. Extend your love and appreciation for Creator, and welcome in your Angelic Friends.

6. Move into the Grounding position. Share your appreciation, and connect to Planet Earth.

7. Move your hands into the Cleansing position. Feel yourself purified and ready for new experiences!

Hand Massage

This activity increases the hand's ability to send out Life Energy. It loosens up and stimulates the hands' abundant nerve endings. Incidentally, there is a relationship between the nerve endings and every part of the body that has been mapped out on hand-reflexology charts.

1. Remove all jewelry and metal from your hands.

2. Loosen and release their physical tension by gently shaking your hands.

3. Stretch your hands and wiggle your fingers.

4. With a gentle pulsing motion, massage every part of your hand: fingers, palms, back of hands, between the fingers, and wrists. Have one hand massage the other, and then switch.

5. Gently stroke your hands from the wrist to fingertips several times. Do this on both sides of your hands.

6. Move your hands into the Perceiving position, and notice how they send out a clearer flow of Life Energy.

7. Rinse your hands in water and give them a fresh start.

You can massage your own hands or exchange hand massages with a friend. There are many hand massaging techniques, this one increases the flow of Life Energy through your hands. Enjoy!

Pumping the Energy Ball

This practice builds the intensity of the Energy Ball by bouncing it within the space between your hands. It starts very slowly and as pressure builds, a spongy sensation is felt, and it becomes springy.

1. With your hands in the Charging position, push them towards each other, compacting and making the Life Energy between them denser.

2. This creates a gentle pressure that wants to expand and push your hands slightly outwards.

3. Allow the pressure to move your hands until they are no longer being pushed.

4. At that moment, feel a tiny bounce of your hands.

5. Move your hands inwards again, until the pressure pushes them outwards as it did before.

6. With each expanding and compacting cycle, notice how the amount and intensity of the Energy Ball becomes thicker and stronger and the bounce has more pressure.

7. Continue with this in-and-out motion, emphasizing the bounce. Do this about 20 times at a rapid pace to develop elasticity in your Energy Ball.

8. Let your body move with the motion, allowing Life Energy to circulate and nourish you.

9. This back and forth rhythm is known as *Pumping the Energy Ball*.

10. Rinse your hands in water after this practice.

Encoding the Energy Ball

Words are potent! They carry vibrations, have meaning, help us communicate, and have creative possibilities. When words are

spoken in a wise and respectful tone their vibration inspires and stimulates us; creating a sacred atmosphere.

In the Energy Ball for Peace Ceremony we use a spoken Blessing. The words that are directed into the Energy Ball infuse it with their vibration. The Energy Ball is then said to be *encoded* with Blessing.

Do the following to practice encoding the Energy Ball:

1. In the Charging position, form an Energy Ball.

2. With a confident voice, say the word, *Respect*, a few times and notice how the vibration of this sacred word affects the Energy Ball.

3. Say the words *Thank You*, and note how this word has a slightly different vibration.

4. What do you notice about the delicate energy between your hands? Can you feel the intensity change? Do you feel a response in your body? These questions assist you to get in touch with the words' vibrational effects.

5. Experiment with other words, and pay close attention to their unique sensations: love, joy, friendship, magical, opening, nature, freedom, sacred, peace. Then say them in

other languages. Notice what happens to the Energy Ball.

6. By saying these words and noticing their vibration, you learn to encode Blessings into the Energy Ball.

7. After you have encoded the Energy Ball, place the Energy Ball around your body[21].

8. Move your hands into the Cleansing position and allow the information Encoded into the Energy Ball to integrate into your body.

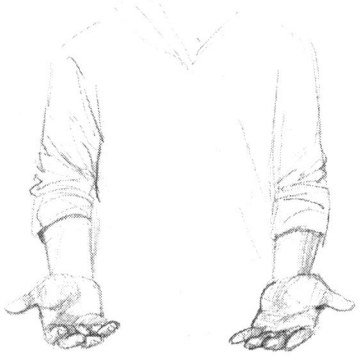

Blowing into the Energy Ball

Blowing air out of your mouth and into the Energy Ball changes the quality and quantity of Life Energy flowing through the Energy Ball.

The amount and speed of the air blown into the Energy Ball changes its vibration as follows:

• A consistent gentle stream of air charges the Energy Ball making it feel thicker and fuller.

• One long and strong powerful burst of air quickly intensifies the Energy Ball, and immediately provides available Life Energy.

---

21 See Blessing yourself with an Elongated Energy Ball, page 52

- A series of strong breaths; inflates the Energy Ball, nourishes your overall energy body, and gives you a secure feeling. Continuing with the strong breaths may bring on a euphoric effect.

Practicing blowing air into the Energy Ball, and notice what effect it has on you and your overall energy body.

Filling up the Energy Ball

The activity fills up the Energy Ball, revitalizes you, and makes you shine!

1. In the Nurturing position, form an Energy Ball.

2. Welcome Life Energy in through the top of your head into your pineal gland. Then visualize the Life Energy spreading out into all your body systems.

3. Invite this increased flow of Life Energy to enter deep into all of the cells in your body, nourishing them, making them smile, and creating happy cells!

4. Notice that the Life Energy goes into and fills up the Energy Ball, and that the Energy Ball intensifies and becomes denser and hotter.

5. Sense how you are overflowing with Life Energy, and how your overall energy body has expanded and become gigantic!

Stimulating the Fingers

This activity stimulates Life Energy channels in your fingers, assisting them to focus.

1. Starting with the index finger on each hand, place your fingertips of each hand opposite one another, about 2-3 cm (1 inch) apart, focusing Life Energy between both fingertips.

2. Describe to yourself what are you sensing between your fingers.

3. Slowly shift to the middle fingers, noting their unique vibration of Life Energy.

4. Continue with your other fingers in the same manner so that you can become acquainted with your fingers' diverse Life Energy flow.

Smiling with the Energy Ball

Smiling happens naturally. It is the result of being happy and feeling good. When smiling bubbles over, it creates laughter. People who pretend to smile, say for a picture, look like they are happy, and this is a beginning.

During the Energy Ball for Peace Ceremony, participants are encouraged to smile at each other. Smiling together opens a window of light that brings hope to humanity. When we smile, the Energy Ball and our body is charged with a spirit of joy!

Practice this activity:

1. In the Charging position, form an Energy Ball and let it build up in intensity.

2. Place the Energy Ball around your jaw, and notice what happens to your smile.

3. Move the Energy Ball so that your fingertips are gracefully following your facial movements.

4. Notice how the Energy Ball relaxes your jaw muscles, and how the feeling of relaxation spreads to your entire body.

5. Move your facial muscles around by accentuating your smile. Then making a very sad face, following with your fingertips. Doing this a few times releases old tension in your face.

6. Look at yourself in the mirror and change the way you smile into a funnier position. Keep trying different facial expressions, allowing your fingertips to follow and dance along.

7. Notice which facial expression and smile pleases you, and remember to look this way.

8. Welcome your Angelic Friends with a Blessing. They love to be around people who are smiling!

Notice how this activity creates a lighter feeling, makes you laugh, and provides a sensation of self-confidence. Smiling is contagious and affects everyone around you!

Energy Ball Using your Feet

I have been instinctively forming Energy Balls with my feet most of my life, but never thought of giving what I was doing a name. While editing the grounding section, I joyfully realized I was forming an Energy Ball with my feet!

Here is an activity to stimulate your feet's nerve endings and open their energy pores.

1. While sitting, place the soles of your bare feet very close to each other, but not touching, in the Perceiving Earth Energy position.

2. Once you sense the energy flow, spread your feet, slightly bend your toes, and form an Energy Ball using your feet.

3. Pay attention to how each foot's nerve endings are stimulated by each other, even tickled.

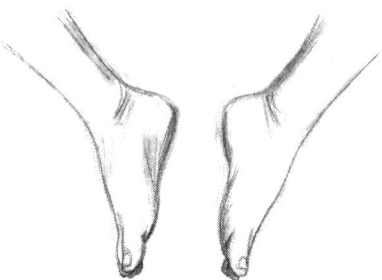

4. The Energy between the feet feels different and stronger than the Energy coming out of the hands. It feels thick and heavy, like soil.

5. Appreciate how Earth energy nurtures your body, feeds the ground, and is available for your utilization. The energy that goes into your body makes you feel solid and present. The energy that goes into the Earth strengthens you on your journey. The energy available may be used as you choose.

6. Say a Blessing of love and appreciation to Creator for your feet, thank Planet Earth for her abundance, and welcome in the spirit of peace.

7. Touch the soles of your feet together to neutralize the energy flow. Then rinse your feet in water, preferably fresh flowing water.

The next step is the Walking Ceremony.[22]

---

22 *See Walking Ceremony, page 189*

Chapter 5: Self-Care

As human beings we are in constant need of continually nurturing ourselves. When this caring includes the Energy Ball, we feel radiant, alive and full of Life Energy.

- Blessing Water and Food
- Grounding
- Self-blessing using an Elongated Energy Ball
- Eyes ~ Mirror ~ Energy Ball
- Adjusting your Overall Energy Body
- Attuning to the Natural World
- Feeding Your Joyfulness!

These self-care activities complement the Energy Ball: breathe fresh air, walk in nature, get plenty of exercise, eat mindfully, rest when needed, be respectful and loving, have daily experiences that stimulate your spirit, create joy in yourself and others, communicate with Creator and your Angelic Friends, learn from every experience, and enjoy life in a variety of ways!

Blessing Water and Food

Encoding with Life Energy and sacred word blessings the water we drink and the food we eat nourishes our body with the spiritual essence of the food and water. This makes the water and food we take in easy to assimilate, and a pleasure for our physical body to receive. The nutrients of the food and water happily enter into our cells, creating a healthier physical body.

- **A ~ Blessing water**
- **B ~ Blessing food**

A ~ Blessing Water

1. Form an Energy Ball in the Charging position and allow time for it to intensify.

2. Surround the water with the energy from the ball. For a glass of water, place your hands around the glass without touching it.

3. Say a Blessing of thankfulness to water. Here is an example:

   "Thank you, water, for your sacred flow! You were once in a cloud, then a raindrop, part of a stream, and somehow you found your way to me! I am so grateful for you and deeply appreciate your abundant gifts to myself and all of Planet Earth."

4. Pay attention to how Life Energy from your hands enters the molecules of water, encoding each one of them with your appreciative light vibration!

5. As you utilize this blessed water, notice that it creates a refreshing and harmonizing experience in and around your body.

 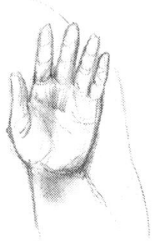

6. If the water you wish to bless is more extensive, for instance a lake or ocean, then use the Radiant position. Allow the Energy from your hands to be extended outwards, surrounding the water with your appreciative Blessing.

B ~ Blessing Food

1. Form an Energy Ball in the Charging position.

2. Place your hands so that they surround the food you are about to eat.

3. Consider the source of the food; a lush vegetable garden, grains blowing in the field, fruit ripening on a tree, and even the giant commercial fields.

4. Sense your thankfulness for the wondrous creation of the food and all that it took to bring it to you: from the hands that gathered it, to the packers, truck drivers, storekeepers and cooks.

5. Say a Blessing to Creator for the nourishment that you are about to ingest:

   "Thank You, Creator, for the sacred food I am about to eat, for its journey to me, and its ability to nourish and enliven the cells of my body, and invigorate my spirit. Thank you for the magic of creation! I am excited about eating food charged with Life Energy!"

6. Envision the cells of the food charged in the light from the Blessed Energy Ball, and any tension, impure or unappreciated vibrations in and around the food purifying.

7. Notice that the energy of your food is vibrant and deeply nourishes your body.

Grounding

These activities, create a stronger and clearer connection between your body and the energy of Planet Earth. They are done before and after Energy Ball activities, and are helpful when you have a floating sensation, or feel you are not connected to the Earth. Used on a consistent basis, these grounding activities keep you balanced and enhance your life quality!

Rinse your hands and feet in water before and after these activities. This helps you to have a more accurate and clearer experience.

- **Activity A** ~ Grounding practice
- **Activity B** ~ Energetic roots
- **Activity C** ~ Connecting to Planet Earth

Activity A ~ Grounding Practice

1. Form an Energy Ball in the Charging position, and allow it to intensify.
2. Turn your hands so that your palms face towards the earth in the Grounding position.
3. Sense Life Energy flowing from your hands into the Planet Earth.
4. Bring your hands closer to the ground and feel the energy coming out of the Planet Earth.
5. Notice how the energy coming out of the Earth feels thicker, and the way in which it affects the density of Life Energy in your body.
6. Raise your hands up to shoulder height, palms still facing downwards, connected to Planet Earth.
7. Notice how your hands receive less Earth energy, and brings a lighter sensation into your body.
8. Control the amount of Earth energy entering inside your body by moving your hands slowly towards the Earth.
9. Stop when it feels you are receiving the correct amount of

Earth energy for you. Remember this distance, and return to this position whenever you feel the need to balance.

Now that you have practiced connecting to Earth energy, pay attention to it wherever you go, learning and experiencing the language of Planet Earth.

Activity B ~ Energetic Roots

This activity connects you directly into Planet Earth by using the image of roots coming out of your feet. With your energy roots, you give and receive Earth energy, nurture Planet Earth, and enliven your body at the same time!

1. Form an Energy Ball in the Grounding position, and notice how this position stabilizes you.

2. Place your bare feet on the ground, and sense what it feels like to be on Planet Earth's surface and connected.

3. Intensify the flow of Life Energy moving through your feet by directing your hands towards them.

4. After you sense a solid connection, guide increased Life Energy to your feet by imagining light entering into your body through the top of your head, and steadily flowing throughout your entire body. Focus on it going through your legs and out the bottom of your feet into the ground.

5. Visualize Life Energy continuing to flow through the pores of your feet, creating very tiny streams that enter into the ground. These streams turn into your *energetic roots*, and integrate with Planet Earth's vibration.

6. To send a rush of Life Energy flowing through your roots, take a strong breath and blow it towards your feet, nurturing Planet Earth.

7. Notice how your connection and perception of what is happening in Planet Earth has increased. Notice also a strong clarification in your entire body's Life Energy flow.

8. You have just fed Planet Earth with light! Thank yourself!

9. Move your hands into the Cleansing position and reaffirm your connection to Creator.

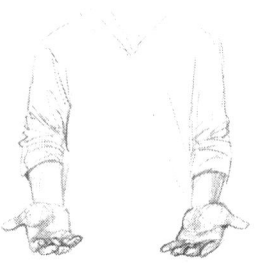

Activity C ~ Connecting to Planet Earth

This activity sends a beam of light to the core of Planet Earth by sending Life Energy through your feet while they are slightly off the ground.

1. Form an Energy Ball with your hands in the Charging position and notice your breath.

2. At the same time, form an Energy Ball with your feet, paying attention to the Earth energy sensation[23].

3. Raise your feet up off the ground about 15 centimeters (6 inches). It helps to put some pillows under your thighs or to use a recliner.

4. Guide Life Energy from the souls of your feet deep into Planet Earth.

5. Then slightly bring your legs and feet out wider, and form a Couple Energy Ball between you and Planet Earth. It feels like you are on top of a horse.

---

23 *See Energy Ball Using your Feet, page 43*

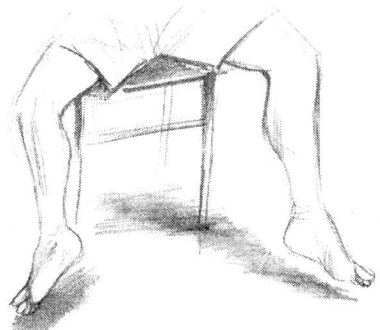

6. Move your hands into the Radiant position, and direct them towards your feet. This increases the intensity of Life Energy flowing through them.

7. Visualize Life Energy from your feet going deeper and deeper into the ground, and turning into a potent ray of light. It penetrates layer after layer of rock and earth until it reaches the core of the Planet Earth.

8. Notice and perceive the waves of Planet Earth inside the Energy Ball.

9. To conclude, say a Blessing of thankfulness for your direct connection to the source of your physical existence, Planet Earth.

10. Rinse your feet in water, and give them a fresh start.

Our feet give and receive energy all the time. Following are some of my thoughts about feet:

- Feet flat on the ground: enables you to perceive the energy coming out of Planet Earth, and send Light Blessings.
- Energy Ball using your feet ~ increases circulation of Earth energy in the body, and nourishes you with a solid vibration[24].
- Feet walking and running ~ stimulates and charges the body by increasing the flow of Life Energy through it.
- Feet resting ~ represents your feet digesting their recent experiences, neutralizing energy – smiling, happy feet.

Self-Blessing using an Elongated Energy Ball

---

24   *See Energy Ball Using your Feet, page 43*

To prepare yourself to have a purer life experience, surround yourself with an elongated Energy Ball. This creates a safe space, where your overall energy body may cleanse and strengthen.

1. Form an Energy Ball in the Charging position, and allow it to build up its intensity with the intention of honoring, Blessing, and nourishing yourself.

2. Bring the Energy Ball above your head. Visualize and sense Life Energy flowing from the ball, moving down and around your body.

3. Slowly move the Energy Ball, first surrounding your head, then slowly downwards to surround your shoulders and chest.

4. Notice that the Energy Ball creates space in the upper part of your body. Notice too how you are being filled with a Blessing of light energy.

5. Continue, moving the Energy Ball so that it surrounds your chest, abdomen and lower back, and then move your hands down to Bless your legs and feet.

6. Pay attention to how there is increasing space inside your body.

7. Do this procedure a few times, each time at a slightly faster pace, following the speed that is correct for you.

8. When finished, rinse your hands in water. Notice that your overall energy body is refreshed!

Eyes ~ Mirror ~ Energy Ball

Looking into your eyes in the mirror is an opportunity for internal communication.

In this activity, the Energy Ball provides a stable vibration while you enter within yourself to organize your internal relationship.

This activity provides you with a way to connect to your spirit and to adjust the way you think about yourself. I like to perform this in the morning, or anytime I wish to focus myself.

1. Form an Energy Ball in the Nurturing position, and direct the ball's energy inwards towards your solar plexus.

2. Notice how your body and spirit connect in this present moment.

3. Look softly and deeply into your eyes in the mirror, and say a Blessing of thankfulness for being in your body and alive on Planet Earth in this moment.

4. Maintain the gaze until you notice a mist appearing around you. Your peripheral vision assists you to see the mist.

5. As you remain with this gaze, an increased connection between your body and spirit happens. Your eyes change what you see, as the vibrations in your body become more organized. This is evidenced by an alive, tingling sensation that is felt in the Energy Ball.

6. Move your hands into the Cleansing position.

7. Notice the lines on your face; each one has a story. Bless and appreciate every one of these experiences. It is a good time for forgiving oneself. If you start to cry, know that this is a genuine release and discharge of old stuck energy. This release is very important for your spiritual development.

8. Allow your vision to see the younger, more alive you, filled with vitality. Remember the way you looked when you were younger, and invite this vibration into your body.

9. Open a communication channel with your spirit and Creator using this Blessing:

   "Thank you, Creator, for this opportunity to be alive in this sacred human form right now in this moment on

Planet Earth! I welcome all of my spirit deep into my body, my mind, and my emotions. Thank you, Creator, for everything. I commit myself to be fully present in my body, and to spread light and peace this day and every day!"

10. Take the Energy Ball and Bless yourself by placing it around your body[25].

11. To conclude, rinse your hands and face with cool water.

Adjusting your Overall Energy Body

In this activity, you change the size of the Energy field around your body using the Energy Ball and your intent.

Adjusting the size of our overall energy body gives us control over the quality of our life, and how we interact with people and circumstances during daily life.

1. Form an Energy Ball in the Charging position.

2. Sense how the Energy Ball is connected to your overall energy body.

3. To contract, slowly move your hands towards each other and at the same time, tell yourself to condense. This brings your overall energy body closer in towards your physical body, and creates a space that feels like a womb – warm, safe and secure.

4. To expand, move your hands away from each other. At the same time, tell yourself to expand. This enlarges your overall energy body. You can allow it to expand as large as you wish, even gigantic!

---

25 *See Self-Blessing, page 52*

5. To find your overall energy body's correct size for this moment, blow a gentle stream of Life Energy into the Energy Ball. Allow your hands to expand with your breath until you intuitively sense what is a comfortable distance for your overall energy body.

6. By giving yourself the thought command of consistency, you bring your overall energy body to this distance.

7. Rinse your hands in water and give them a fresh start!

Attuning to the Natural World

The physical body of the human beings is part of the natural world. When we are in a natural environment, our internal natural instincts are stimulated. Consistent visits or living in a natural environment reminds the physical body of its natural cycles.

Living in the covered-over natural environment of a city or suburbs confuses the natural instincts, and causes complications in the physical body.

Therefore, frequent visits to the natural world are vital! Nature provides countless opportunities for our natural instincts to be stimulated, and for us to remember that we are *natural* human beings.

In these activities, the Energy Ball takes you on a journey as you receive nature's nourishment.

A ~ Returning to Nature

B ~ Arriving in Nature

C ~ Integrating with Nature

D ~ Blending with a Tree

E ~ Bringing Natural Vibration back to the City

A ~ Returning to Nature

When people become accustomed to city and suburban life, and then go out into nature, their bodies require time to adjust and tune into the sacred setting.

Use the following activity to transition out of suburbia, and to develop a deeper, stronger, integrative experience with nature.

1. Know your timeframe before you leave, so you are not rushed during your adventure. Don't forget to put your cell phone on silent so you are not disturbed.

2. Before leaving, form an Energy Ball in the Nurturing position.

3. Close your eyes and envision yourself traveling to and arriving at your natural destination.

4. Say a Blessing, and welcome Creator and your Angelic Friends to join you on your upcoming journey.

5. Bless yourself and your upcoming journey by placing the Energy Ball, encoded with your intention, around yourself and your transportation to the natural world.

6. On your way, out of suburbia appreciate nature inside the city, noticing everything that is natural around you.

7. Sense how it affects you. Do you feel intrigued and excited to touch some authentic nature? Express it with some words or song as you travel.

B ~ Arriving in Nature

1. When you arrive in nature, form an Energy Ball in the Perceiving position.

2. Look around you and pay attention to the vegetation, sky, Sun, and everything natural such as trees, rock formations, animals, plants, insects, etc. Sense how their unique vibrations affect the Energy Ball.

3. Listen to birds singing, water moving, wind blowing through the trees, and the smell of the air. Invite these sensations into the Energy Ball by saying what you are sensing, seeing, and hearing out loud, and directing their specific vibrations into the Energy Ball.

4. Change your hands into the Radiant position.

5. Send Life Energy to each aspect of nature, and express your

appreciation by saying a Blessing.

6. Notice that your Blessing is received. Instantly, a feeling-sensation returns, stimulating your natural instincts.

7. Open yourself further by taking a deep breath and smelling nature's fragrance.

8. Place the Energy Ball around your body, noticing how it integrates with your overall energy body. Natural energy blends with your Life Energy flow, feeding the natural part of you.

9. Go over and touch whichever part of nature calls you. Give it your love and deep appreciation.

10. Investigate, explore, and integrate with the natural world, and its colors and textures.

C ~ Integrating with Nature

1. Creating an Energy Ball in the Charging position, and look into it deeply with the intent of connecting more intimately with the natural world.

2. Say a Blessing of thankfulness for being in sacred nature. Welcome Creator and Angels to join you.

3. Once again, look at everything natural around you. This time, pay attention to the intricacies and life essence of the trees, birds, animals, insects, rocks, plants, flowers, butterflies, sky, moon, stars, clouds, and other things. Continue this for a few minutes, taking your time and genuinely looking at and appreciating the variety of the natural world.

4. Sense how their pure, natural essences charge the energy between your hands into a natural vibration.

5. Invite these essences to integrate with you by placing the Energy Ball around your body and Blessing yourself.

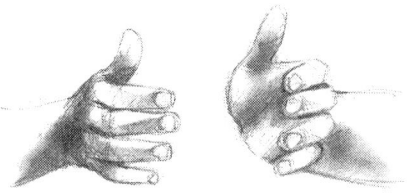

6. Using the Radiant position, direct the energy from your hands to each aspect of nature while you speak to them out loud.

7. Notice how focused Life Energy from your hands connects you to them. Pay attention to how each part of nature has a unique vibration.

8. Tune into the message that nature is gives back to you. Receive the information through your hands, and check if it is familiar or means something special to you. This tuning in and observation assist you in blending with nature.

9. Move your hands into the Cleansing position for as long as you wish, and feel yourself renewed.

10. How does it feel to be connected and at one with nature? Write about it.

D ~ Blending with a Tree

Trees stimulate the thinking process, and open the doorway to wisdom. Combined with the Energy Ball, we welcome this wisdom deeper into our thought process[26].

Thoughts to consider:

- It is natural to blend with a tree's energy, simply requiring respect and thankfulness.

- When creating an Energy Ball with a tree, notice how the tree's energy envelops you.

- When you form an Energy Ball sitting next to or on a tree, you create a solid energetic bond. The evidence is that it is hard to separate from the tree. You feel rooted and part of the tree and Planet Earth.

- When you approach a tree, acknowledge the vital connection you have regarding the production of oxygen and carbon dioxide. Take several deep breaths with appreciation for oxygen, and notice how it affects the Energy Ball.

---

26   See Umbrella of Light, page 106

- Before you hug, touch or climb a tree, begin by approaching it with the Energy Ball and honoring the sacred tree. Ask the tree if it needs something, and if it is alright for you to climb on its branches and to pick its fruits.

- With the Energy Ball, send Blessings through the tree and its roots to the core of Planet Earth,

- Blending with a tree creates an eternal bond. Some of your human energy and the tree's energy intertwine.

E ~ Bringing Natural Vibration Back to the City

After you have touched the purity of nature and before returning to cars, roads, and buildings, perform this activity:

1. Form an Energy Ball in the Nurturing position.

2. Recall the sensations from a few of the experiences you just had. Note how these sensations make you feel like a natural human being!

3. Express yourself by noticing these sensations, and directing these feelings in spoken or sung words into the Energy Ball. Then continue with an appreciative Blessing:

    "Thank you, nature, for your innate magic and the opportunity I have today to integrate with this ancient essence and feed my natural self. Being here today helps me remember that I am a natural human being! As I leave, I give you this Energy Ball as a gift of my love and deep thankfulness for my experience today!"

4. Open your hands facing outwards in the Radiant position, and walk around in a 360-degree circle, allowing the Energy Ball to spread and Bless all your surroundings[27].

---

27   *See Ceremony to Bless Humanity, page 184*

5. Form another Energy Ball, holding it in the Charging position. Bring your attention to your transportation out of the natural area, surrounding and Blessing it with the Energy Ball.

6. Move your hands into the Cleansing position and say another Blessing:

> *"I acknowledge that modern society has made it possible for me to arrive here today. I recognize that even though human beings cause enormous amounts of harm to the natural world, sacred pure natural space still exists! I am so very, very thankful to have the opportunity to be here today! As I leave, I bring the natural world's message of purity and peace back to modern society and all those I encounter. Thank you, Creator, for your magnificent creation!"*

Feeding Your Joyfulness!

Spreading joy is a mitzvah (good deed)! This activity stimulates joyful emotions, and helps them to spread throughout your body and humanity.

1. Write a list of activities that bring you joy, guide you into your inner healing space, and remind you of your true self. For example, playing with a child, walking in nature, watching a Sunrise or Sunset, tasting nourishing food, enjoying positive relationships with family and friends, learning 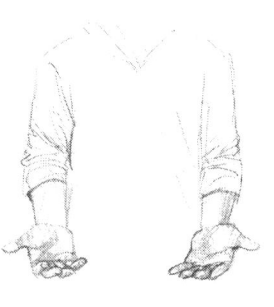 something new, discovering, adventuring, and others.

2. Form an Energy Ball and hold it in the Charging position.

3. Encode the ball with these joyful thoughts by reading your list out loud, and directing your words into the Energy Ball with feeling! This encodes the ball with these joyful thoughts. Go slowly, focusing on one activity at a time.

4. After completing your list, choose one activity, and imagine yourself joyfully having this experience.

5. Notice that the Energy Ball joyously tingles and makes you smile and laugh. It reminds and stimulates your body, making you feel enlivened!

6. Bless yourself by guiding the Energy Ball with its joyful vibration into your body.

7. Allow the Energy Ball to get very large and expand around your body by using a consistent series of breaths. This fills your overall energy body with a joyful vibration, creating a euphoric effect!

8. To go deeper, guide the joyful Energy Ball allowing it to expand around your arms and upper body. This opens your chest and enhances your ability to feel happiness!

9. Visualize yourself as a joyful, beautiful butterfly, gracefully flapping your arms as if they were wings, making you smile, laugh and transform into a joyful person!

10. Move your hands into the Cleansing position, and reaffirm your connection with Creator through an inner Blessing.

11. When you are finished, consciously do some of the activities that bring you joy such as singing, walking in nature, writing, philosophizing, drawing, to name a few.

If it is difficult for you to be joyful, notice where you feel blocked in your body. This is usually around your heart, throat, or abdomen. Place the Energy Ball around this location, breathe into it, and request of yourself to put this sadness on the side so that you can experience happiness now.

Say some words of forgiveness. Then think about your joyful experiences. With your intention and your will power, release this stuck sadness from your body, and choose to become a joyful human being! Then do the *Filling up the Energy Ball* activity[28].

News Flash! The Happiness Index Skyrocketed!!!

It is official!

The index proved that human beings are happier now than at any other time in recorded history. They are also healthier, more caring and loving; plus, they live longer and have more friends!!

The researchers began to inquire about what caused this dramatic shift in the happiness index. They sent out questionnaires, and the responses startled them! There was a large increase in people forming Energy Balls!

When asked why they made the Energy Ball the reasons were from A-Z! Most people said "The Energy Ball makes me feel complete. It helps me remain strong, empowering me to overcome whatever comes my way!" or "The Energy Ball is a way to dissolve negative vibrations that uncaring people create."

Further research revealed that the usage of the Energy Ball was spreading throughout most of the cultures of the world, resulting in less diseases and a healthy relationship with Planet Earth's resources.

There is great optimism for the future of humankind becoming

---

28   *See Filling up the Energy Ball, Page 41*

a peaceful, respectful species on the Planet.

The expectation: the happiness index will keep rising, creating thrilled investors because the new holistic economy is booming!

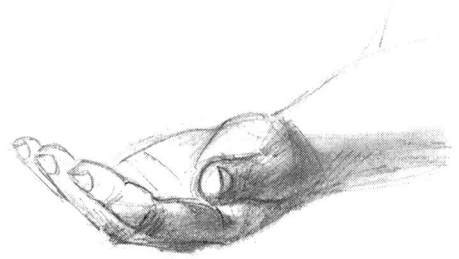

Section 3: Collective Peace Ceremony

Chapter 6: Collective Information

- Collective Ceremony
- Peace Team
- Collective Ceremony Procedure

Collective Ceremony

The *Energy Ball for Peace Ceremony* invites individuals to blend together as a radiant Peace Team.

The ceremony is usually done sitting or standing in a circle so that participants can see one another. There is a leader who guides the participants into a collective team. The goal is to consciously merge and harmonize, providing exponential amounts of light. This collective energy is then sent out in Blessing to humanity and the Planet Earth.

The benefits for the participants are that their body-spirit connection is stimulated, and they each receive the personal Blessing of an increased amount of Life Energy flowing through their bodies.

The leader has assistants who help the participants with sensing the Energy Ball, and organizing teams. Sometimes people are unable or unsure whether they wish to participate. If this is the case, a person can become an observer and send out peace and Light Blessings from the side.

There may be a specific purpose for the ceremony, such as Blessing the Middle East, honoring Planet Earth, loving children, Blessing humanity, nurturing the participants, caring for a situation in the world, and others.

Peace Team

When two or more people come near one another physically, their overall energy bodies begin the process of connecting and interacting. This blending happens quite naturally, creating a collective energy field.

The Energy Ball for Peace Ceremony uses this knowledge to create and send out a clear and strong peaceful vibration.

When the participants harmonize in a conscious way such as the Energy Ball for Peace Ceremony, a sacred, potent vibration is created. I call the people that help create this glorious experience a Peace Team!

Collective Ceremony Procedure

The leader guides the participants through the following phases:

1. Learning to form the Energy Ball and becoming familiar with its sensations.
2. Merging two Energy Balls to form a Couple Energy Ball.
3. Switching partners and meeting other participants.
4. Forming progressive teams of 4, 8, or 16 Energy Balls.
5. Creating one circle with the Collective Energy Ball in the center.
6. Encoding the Collective Energy Ball with Blessings.
7. Lifting the Collective Energy Ball, and releasing it in a ceremonious way.

Chapter 7: Peace Ceremony Tasks

- Peace Ceremony Organizer
- Peace Ceremony Leader
- Peace Ceremony Assistants
- Peace Ceremony Participants
- Peace Ceremony Observers

Peace Ceremony Organizer

The Energy Ball for Peace Ceremony cannot take place without an organizer or a team of organizers[29].

I have done this sacred task many times and have found it to be very spiritually fulfilling, and often exhilarating. It is not very complicated. Here is what you do:

- Choose a time and location.
- Choose a leader or team of leaders.
- Enlist peace ceremony assistants.

Prepare a list of people to invite. Hold the intention that those who really wish to participate and stimulate the spirit of peace will attend. Remember that organizing people is not always easy because of logistics and prior commitments. If the time is inconvenient for some people, invite them to join from a distance.

For an existing group, if there are individuals who are not ready, or unsure about the Energy Ball for Peace Ceremony, invite them to become an observer. They can join in later if they wish.

---

29   See *Organize a Collective Energy Ball for Peace Ceremony page 203*

Use the following or a similar invitation:

Creating Peace Teams
The Energy Ball for Peace Ceremony

Location and date

Please join us in Blessing humanity and stimulating the atmosphere of peace by sending a burst of light into our world!

This ceremony uses the energy coming out of our hands, hearts, and bodies to form a group energy circle. We then infuse this collective energy with our Blessings, and release this sacred vibration in a ceremonious way.

The outcome honors Planet Earth, and forms a Peace Team!

We welcome participants of all ages, including children.

Peace Ceremony Leader

Being the leader of an Energy Ball for Peace Ceremony is a very sacred and stimulating job.

Every Energy Ball for Peace Ceremony is different, depending on the people who show up, the location, weather, time of year, and purpose of the ceremony. Sometimes peace ceremonies are very quiet and meditative, and at other times vibrant and expansive. The key as the leader is to hold a safe space and guide the participants in the creation of a vibrant Collective Energy Ball.

If you are considering becoming a Leader, read over the script several times and consider if you have the following abilities.

If you do not have them all, leading a few Ceremonies will help you develop them.

- Feeling the flow of energy in your hands, and giving simultaneous instructions.
- Projecting confidence, assurance and a positive emotional atmosphere.
- Being aware of how individuals sense and respond to the Energy Ball.
- Staying clear and present for everyone in the ceremony.
- Focusing on clear positive energy, and not getting distracted by impure and chaotic vibrations.

The following considerations are also helpful:

- A Sacred Peace Ceremony is created when you are prepared.
- Practice the Energy Ball and become familiar with all the phases of the ceremony.
- Follow the step-by-step procedure in the leader's script.
- Keep the explanations brief. After the ceremony, there can be more discussion in the talking circle with the Energy Ball[30].
- Remember to maintain the integrity of the Energy Ball throughout the ceremony.
- Some participants may not feel the energy coming out of their hands. You and your assistants help them with the opening hand sensations activity[31].
- Beforehand, have a meeting with your assistants and give them a short review of the ceremony. Then ask them to disperse themselves evenly throughout the group.

---

30   See Talking Circle with the Energy Ball, Page 103
31   See Opening Hand Sensations, Page 23

- If any group has difficulty coming together as a team, bring in one of your assistants.

An Analogy:

Imagine yourself conducting an instrumental orchestra, using the Energy Ball as your baton. It allows you to connect to each person, and assists you in creating a harmonious group vibration.

With your baton, your Energy Ball, you monitor the vibrational changes during each phase of the ceremony. You remind the participants to stay present and in tune with the collective energy and to hold the Energy Ball.

During the Peace Ceremony:

- Observe how the collective energy flows, notice the group's mood, and sense how you can influence them to create a sacred, joyful atmosphere.
- Pay attention to how confident and comfortable each participant is with the Energy Ball. Note which individuals easily feel the Energy Ball and, if you need, ask them to be an assistant.
- After helping a participant to feel the Energy Ball, find one of your assistants, or another person who feels the Energy Ball easily, and ask them to continue with this person. This makes you available for the group.
- When participants form small teams, you and your assistants go around to each group and help them in forming the Collective Energy Ball. I enjoy this part very much!
- Some teams may feel the collective energy quickly, and immediately start to create with it. Other groups may need your help to focus the energy.

- Sometimes it is challenging for the group to maintain the collective energy, and at other times the group easily blends together. Your awareness is the first step in overcoming the challenge.

- To contain the energy of a group, ask everyone to take one step towards the center of the circle. This condenses the Collective Energy Ball into a smaller space, and allows it to be felt and encoded more easily.

- If someone leaves the circle, encourage them to add their Blessing from the side and become an observer.

- When forming teams, if there are an odd number of participants, one group will have an extra person.

One of the benefits of conducting an Energy Ball for Peace Ceremony is that your perceptive abilities expand.

Peace Ceremony Assistants

Anyone who feels confident with the Energy Ball and wishes to help the leader may volunteer to be an assistant. I love having assistants. They increase the collective agreement, and make containing the group easier. Also, they notice what I cannot observe, especially with large groups.

Peace ceremony assistants:

- Notice the overall energy of the group.

- Hold a Sacred Space for the Peace Ceremony.

- Help participants to sense the Energy Ball.

- Lead and organize small teams.

- Bring joy, radiance, assurance, love and appreciation into the ceremony.

Peace Ceremony Participants

The participants are the foundation of the Peace Ceremony. Each participant is instructed how to form an Energy Ball, form small teams, and merge into the collective circle.

A few thoughts for the participants:

- Maintain the integrity of the Energy Ball throughout the ceremony.

- Enable the leader to guide you into teams.

- When connecting with a partner or group, be sensitive. Gently bring your Energy Ball to them, blending and merging together.

- Remember that the Energy Ball is a very sacred, spiritual vibration. Playfully tossing or throwing the Energy Ball can dissipate this gentle substance. It is best to move the Energy Ball with care, wisdom and joy.

- If, at any time during the Peace Ceremony, you lose the sensation in your hands, return to the Perceiving position. If needed, ask for help.

- If you see someone who needs help in sensing the Energy Ball, and you feel confident, help them or find an assistant to help them.

- The Energy Ball for Peace Ceremony is a non-touch activity. Be conscious and respectful of the personal as well as cultural boundaries of other participants.

- Many participants turn into Peace People after the ceremony, choosing to spread their light and peaceful vibrations with confidence.

- Those people who are unsure whether or not they wish to form an Energy Ball with the group may choose to hold their Energy Ball by themselves on the side and become an observer.

The Energy Ball for Peace Ceremony is a strong experience and can be challenging to handle for those who have had psychological problems. If you are on psychiatric medication, ask your doctor if the Energy Ball for Peace Ceremony is good for you.

Peace Ceremony Observers

The observers provide energetic support from the side, assisting with their Blessings of peace. Observers may choose to hold the Energy Ball by themselves and join the group any time they wish.

Chapter 8
Phases of the Peace Ceremony

- Forming the Energy Ball
- Couple Energy Balls
- Eye Gazing
- Sharing with a Partner
- Building Phase ~ Teams of Four
- Teams of Eight
- Being in the Middle of the Circle
- Collective Team
- Ceremony Blessings
- Releasing the Collective Energy Ball
- Concluding the Ceremony

Forming the Energy Ball

Participants are guided by the leader through the process of creating the Energy Ball. Once they form the Energy Ball, each one focuses on the spirit of inner peace and becomes acquainted with the Energy Ball's sensations.

Couple Energy Balls

Two participants join their Energy Balls together, and experience what it feels like to share an Energy Ball with another person.

Participants change partners according to the leader's instructions. This provides everyone an opportunity to meet one another. Participants are asked to gaze into the eyes of their partner and share a few words about what they are sensing in their hands.

Eye Gazing

There is a saying that the *eyes are the gateway to the soul*, and I agree!

Eye gazing and the Energy Ball are excellent partners as they open a clear channel in both participants and create potent collective energy. The results of eye gazing can range from a casual connection to a very powerful life-long relationship!

During the Energy Ball for Peace Ceremony, we utilize eye gazing to deepen spiritual connection.

Looking into someone's eyes can be a very intimate experience, therefore, not everyone is comfortable with eye gazing, so do not insist on looking into your partner's eyes.

Sharing with a Partner

Participants talk together about their experience with the Energy Ball. This assists them to clarify their experience and meet other participants.

One person says their name, and briefly describes the sensations that they are experiencing between their hands. Their partner actively listens, maintaining the integrity of the Couple Energy Ball.

Sometimes there are no words to complement this vibration and the couple communicates in silence.

Building Phase ~ Teams of Four

Two couple teams blend together to form a stronger and more versatile Collective Energy Ball. This creates an increase in Life Energy circulation in the participants' bodies, accentuating peaceful and joyful emotions! Hands are held in the Charging or Radiant positions with the Collective Energy Ball in the center.

By making eye contact with each member of your team, an energetic web is created, fortifying your collective energy.

Each team's experience will be unique. It may be expansive, dynamic, intense with lots of fun and laughter, or quiet and meditative. It can also be a deep healing experience for one or more members of the team.

Teams of Eight

When two teams of four merge together, a chain reaction of light is created that has enormous potential!

Hands are in the Radiant position. Participants take one step backwards and create a larger space, where any participant who wishes goes into the center of the circle and experiences the collective light energy.

Being in the Middle of the Circle

There is an intensified energy field in the center of the circle. This is an opportunity for individual expansion, cleansing and spiritual growth. The leader invites anyone who wishes to go into the center of the circle. Participants choose for themselves when and if to enter.

The rest of the group holds their hands in the Radiant position, providing a safe space. The length of time a person stays in the center varies; it is usually about one minute. Not everyone has to enter. In the center of the circle, the individual is bathed in and blessed with Life Energy from the Collective Energy Ball. During this intensified experience, the receiver's overall energy body clears and adjusts itself, and their senses are stimulated!

I love to be in the center, and to feel surrounded and blessed by layers of nurturing and warm radiant Sunlight.

Collective Team

The entire group merges together, forming the collective team.

Coming together is sometimes a challenge because the Energy Ball is delicate, and often people move too quickly. Therefore, the leader or an assistant guides the teams of 8 to a central group.

It is important for each participant to be mindful of maintaining the integrity of the Energy Ball during the merging. As each group joins, there is a noticeable increase in the intensity of the Collective Energy Ball.

After all the groups have joined in, the participants stand side by side in a circle, with their hands facing towards the center in the Radiant position. They hold the Collective Energy Ball in the center of the circle.

When everyone comes together into one circle, a wave of intensified Life Energy circulates in and around all the participants, creating a sensation of oneness!

Ceremony Blessings

Once the collective team has come together, it is time to encode the Collective Energy Ball with peaceful, loving, respectful vibrations. This is done in the form of word Blessings.

The Blessing includes:

• Appreciation to Creator and our Angelic Friends.

• Thankfulness for our opportunity to be in this present moment participating in the peace ceremony.

• Conscious desire and intention to send forth healing light to our world.

• Hopes and prayers for human beings becoming excellent caretakers of Planet Earth[32].

Sometimes there are a specific purpose for the ceremony, such as Blessing the Middle East.

The leader offers the initial Blessing and then invites other participants who speak different languages and are from other religions and cultures, to share a few sacred words. These words infuse the Collective Energy Ball with a multicultural, interreligious, and international vibration.

---

32   *See Ceremony to Hug Planet Earth Planet, page 182*

Releasing the Collective Energy Ball

The leader guides the collective team to release and spread out the Blessed Energy Ball. This is done by the group gathering the energy into one condensed Energy Ball and then lifting it up into the atmosphere. Once released, it is escorted by Angelic Friends.

Concluding the Peace Ceremony

After being together in one collective energy body and sending out Blessings, it is important to transition back into your own overall energy body.

Participants find a place where they are not near another person, and move their hands into the Cleansing position[33]. They imagine light energy as water flowing in and around their body, purifying them. For the full version go to the *Waterfall of Liquid Light* activity[34]. Afterwards, they rinse their hands in water.

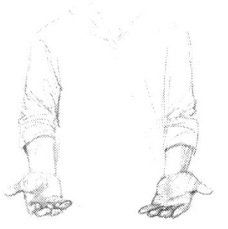

---

33 *See Cleansing Position, page 29*
34 *See Waterfall of Liquid Light, page 21*

Chapter 9: Peace Ceremony Script

The leader reads the indented script. In preparation, the leader requests participants to remove and put in a safe place objects such as silenced mobile phones, jewelry, watches, and any other metal objects. The leader also requests that participants rinse their hands in water before and after the peace ceremony.

> *Welcome and thank you for coming to the Energy Ball for Peace Ceremony! We now have an opportunity to merge together as a Peace Team, and send out a large burst of Life Energy filled with Blessings and prayers for peace into our world!*
>
> *To accomplish this, we utilize the Life Energy coming out of our hands and form what is called an Energy Ball. Then you will be invited to share your Energy Ball with other participants in progressive teams of 2, 4, 8. Eventually, we will come together into one circle.*
>
> *Once we are in a circle, we encode the Collective Energy Ball with Blessings of peace, love, light, joy, and our hope and prayers that all human beings may awaken and are inspired by the vibration of peace.*
>
> *Then the Collective Energy Ball is released into the atmosphere, spreading our peaceful intentions with the help of our Angelic Friends.*
>
> *Assistants, please raise your hands. If you need help, ask one of them. Thank you!*
>
> *So, let's get started! Please follow me.*

Demonstrate the following while saying to the group:

> *Let's begin with gently shaking our hands, loosening*

them. This allows Life Energy to flow through them more easily.

*Look at your marvelous, wonderful, amazing HANDS! They do so many vital activities: dress you, feed you, and care for you in every way. They write, create, dance, play music, drive, climb, build, tinker, assist others......
Genuinely appreciate this amazing part of your body!*

Move your fingers in tiny motions, noticing how easily they respond. As we pay attention to our hands, an important conscious connection is created allowing increased Life Energy to flow out of them.

If you do not have the use of your hands, use the Visualizing the Energy Ball activity[35].

Give the participants about one minute to connect to their hands. Be aware when the group is ready to move on and then say:

Place your hands very close together, almost touching, and pay attention to what happens between them. Notice what type of sensation you are feeling. It can be a gentle pressure, warmth, heat, a flowing and tingling sensation or a magnetic feeling. Maintain this position and realize that right now you are sensing Life Energy! This is called the Perceiving position. If at any time during the ceremony you no longer feel the sensation in

---

35   *See Visualizing the Energy Ball, page 22*

your hands, go back to this position.

Now slightly bend your fingers and palms, forming them into a round shape. Sense how Life Energy comes out of your hands and is condensed into a circular form.

Notice that you have just made an Energy Ball! Simple and actual!

Allow the Energy Ball to build its integrity and intensity by moving your hands close to each other and then further apart. Doing this several times pumps the Energy Ball and helps Life Energy to solidify.

Give the participants sufficient time to become familiar with the Energy Ball. When you sense that most people are ready, move to the next step of forming Couple Energy Balls.

Say and demonstrate the following procedure with an assistant:

Now we are going to form Couple Energy Balls. Turn to the person next to you and slightly spread your hands, allowing both of your Energy Balls to merge and blend together.

You and your assistants should make sure each participant finds a partner.

After about a minute, say:

We are going to switch partners now, so please gently and carefully bring your Energy Ball to another person, and allow them to merge.

During this Couple Energy Ball, you are invited to connect to your partner deeper by gazing into their eyes and making a spiritual connection[36]. This can be a very profound experience.

For those who are uncomfortable with eye gazing, you may skip this part.

After a minute or so, again invite them to switch partners by saying:

Find a new person to form a Couple Energy Ball with. This time, share your name and what you are sensing between your hands and in your body. Use just a few words[37].

During the next couple sharing, request that everyone be silent and utilize this time for inner connection, Blessing and prayer.

Continue forming new Couple Energy Balls until most of the participants have met one another. Pay careful attention to how the group energy is building. The next step is to form teams of four people, say:

---

36 *See Eye Gazing, page 78*
37 *See Sharing with Partner page 78*

Now that you have met one another, let's build the Collective Energy Ball by merging into teams of four people. To make the process smoother, slightly compress your Couple Energy Ball, locate a couple near you, and gently bring your two Couple Energy Balls together. Pay attention to maintain the integrity of the Energy Ball while moving to another team.

Once you are in teams of four, notice how the Collective Energy Ball changes and has a life of its own. Sometimes it expands to become very large and at other times, it brings joy and makes you laugh. It can also shrink into a tiny Energy Ball and become very hot! Sense what your team's Energy Ball wants to do.

You and your assistants help to form the teams. Then move from team to team, noticing how you can assist each group's vibration to more smoothly blend together. Use your smile combined with the Energy Ball and very few words. Enjoy the experience of witnessing the participants as their Life Energy flows and their hearts open. Some of the teams may become playful and lighten up the entire group atmosphere. When a group starts to laugh, I laugh with them and encourage others to join in!

To move into the next phase, say:

We are now going to expand into teams of 8. While forming your new group, move slowly and focus on maintaining the integrity of the Collective Energy Ball and making it stronger.

Once the Teams of eight are formed, use the *Being in Middle of the Circle* activity[38].

38　*See Being in Middle of the Circle page 80*

Now that we are in a larger group, I invite one person to go into the center of their circle and be surrounded and blessed by the Team's focused Life Energy. The rest of us will hold our hands facing outwards in the Radiant position. This creates a womb-like space for them to be wrapped in layers of Life Energy.

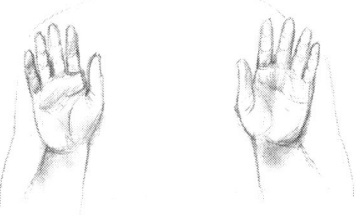

In the center of the circle, there is an intensified energy field. When you are in the middle, allow yourself to experience and feel the Energy Ball surrounding and Blessing your entire body. You may stand still, move around, or dance. Your eyes may be opened or closed. After about a minute or so, I will say "it's time to change the person in the middle," and someone else steps in. Please allow individuals to choose for themselves who goes into the center.

Pay attention to when the group is ready for the Collective Team to merge into one and then say:

> Now we will join together group by group to form one energy circle. To make the process smoother, stay in your team until an assistant or I lead you to the main circle.

Start by leading your team slowly and steadily to the group nearest you. Continue with each team in the same manner until all the participants are in one circle, then say:

> Notice that we are now holding a large Energy Ball in the middle of the circle! It contains our collective radiant light! Let's take a few moments and enjoy the experience.

Give the group a minute or two for silence and then continue:

> As a team, let's move our hands towards the center of the circle and gently push the Collective Energy Ball inwards. Notice how its pressure slightly wants to push your hands outwards.
>
> Now, take a focused step forwards and sense how the Collective Ball continues to compact.
>
> To intensify the Collective Energy Ball even more, I invite you to close your eyes and join me in this short-guided visualization:
>
> Imagine Life Energy entering into your body through the top of your head, into your pineal gland, and then flowing through your entire body enlivening it! Guide this increased flow of Life Energy out of your hands and intensify the Energy Ball.

Give them a few minutes and then say:

> Now that the Collective Energy Ball has intensified, we encode our sacred creation with peace, love, light and hope. We do this by using focused words in the form of a

Blessing. These words are like seeds of peace:

"We thank you, Creator, for this present moment in eternity and for all that is present in our lives: our families, friends, homes, and this sacred Planet upon which we live. We are abundantly thankful for the Sun that nurtures us, and this entire magnificent creation!

As a Peace Team we come together, prepared and ready to send out a burst of radiant light that is filled with respect, love, compassion, trust, vision and hope. Our intention is that we may assist humanity to quickly wake up and return to a peaceful state of coexistence!

As a collective, we welcome in our Angelic Friends and appreciate their assistance in spreading our peaceful vibrations.

We dedicate ourselves to peace, love, joy, happiness, and to the vision of humankind living in a sacred pure reality.

Thank you, Creator."

After the Collective Energy Ball is encoded with Blessings, the next step is to lift it up and spread this peaceful vibration, saying:

We are going to raise up our Collective Energy Ball into the atmosphere so that it may spread its peaceful Blessings!

Demonstrate and explain the following:

Take a step forward, bend down, and with your fingers spread out, gather the energy together with several inward and upward sweeping motions of your hands.

Then place your hands under the Collective Energy Ball, and slowly raise it up to shoulder height.

Wait until all the participants are ready and then say:

The Collective Energy Ball for Peace is ready to be lifted upwards and released into the Earth's atmosphere where it will be guided by our Angelic Friends, with its sacred Blessings and healing power, as a gift of peace to all of creation.

On the count of three, we will release and spread the Collective Energy Ball, with a slight jump and an upwards thrusting motion of the arms.

After we release the Energy Ball,

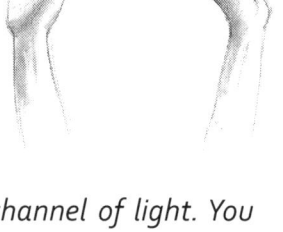

keep your arms and hands facing upwards in the Light Connection position, and experience being a channel of light. You may hold this position for as long as you wish.

Are you ready?

One, Two, Three........

In unison, everyone bends down, gathers the energy, raises it up and joyously releases the Collective Energy Ball for Peace with a slight jump!

After it is released, participants are invited to return to their own overall energy body by using this short version of the *Waterfall of Liquid Light* [39] activity:

> *Please find a place where you are not near anyone else. With your palms facing upward in the Cleansing position, visualize yourself under a waterfall of liquid light that flows around and through your body, cleansing your cells, and renewing your overall energy body.*

A few words to say in conclusion of the Ceremony:

> *The Energy Ball is your friend. Use it whenever you wish to bring in a calming vibration, make a spiritual connection, need a little assistance, or feel you want to bring the vibration of Peace to the atmosphere around you. There are many uses for the Energy Ball both individually and in groups. Enjoy the adventure!*

Invite the group to continue with the collective activities as listed in the next chapter.

39　*See Waterfall of Liquid Light, page 21*

Chapter 10: Collective Activities

These collective activities assist participants to work together as a team. They develop individual relationships and enhance the collective light created during the Energy Ball for Peace Ceremony. Choose from the following list the activities that best fit your group:

- Naming Ceremony
- Collective Chanting
- Sweeping the Overall Energy Body
- Energy Ball Hug
- Sun Rays Blessing Humanity
- Passing the Energy Ball
- Talking Circle with the Energy Ball
- Umbrella of Light ~ Tree Blessing
- Collective Blessing of Food
- Collective Dancing

Participants are encouraged to rinse their hands in water before and after the Energy Ball activities.

Naming Ceremony

This activity acknowledges, honors and blesses each participant as they present themselves before the group.

1. Participants form a Collective Energy Ball using the Radiant position, thereby creating a safe space in the center of the circle.

2. The leader starts as an example and enters the center, looks around at the other participants, receives

their collective light and says their name. They express themselves in any way they wish: simply, dramatically or even singing their name! They may say a phrase that captures an emotion or quality of life that they sense in the moment. The length of time each one speaks is decided by the group beforehand.

3. The person to the leader's left then enters the center of the circle, and presents himself or herself before the group. This process continues, until all the participants have had the chance to introduce themselves.

4. An option is to acknowledge the person in the center by all the participants repeating or singing the person's name.

5. Continue with other collective activities.

Collective Chanting

Forming an Energy Ball while chanting greatly magnifies the vibration of Life Energy.

There are many, many traditions and ways of chanting, from all cultures. These simple chants easily integrate with the Energy Ball for Peace Ceremony.

- **Part A** ~ Individual Toning
- **Part B** ~ Group Harmony
- **Part C** ~ Wave of Peace

Part A ~ Individual Toning

The leader reads the Toning and the Energy Ball explanation and then they do the activity[40].

---

40   *See Toning and the Energy Ball, page 161.*

Part B ~ Group Harmony

The group holds the Energy Ball in the Radiant position and chants into the center of the circle, creating group harmony.

1. The leader starts the chanting with the vowel sound *aaaaa*.

2. The participants listen and then join in harmonizing with

    this tone.

3. After a short while, the leader changes over to a different vowel sound (a, e, i, o, u).

4. The participants follow, sensing which vowel sound feels correct for them to chant in the moment.

5. As the chanting continues, the individual tones blend together creating a group melody.

6. The Collective Energy Ball is Blessed and then released and guided by Angelic Friends.

Part C ~ Wave of Peace

This chant is repeated over and over, charging the Collective Energy Ball with Peace!

1. The group holds the Energy Ball in the Radiant position.

2. The leader guides the group through chanting the word Peace in:

    • Hebrew: *Shalommmm.*

    • Arabic: *Salammmm.*

- English: *Peeeeace.*
- Add other languages.

3. With each round, the participants focus on radiating the vibration of peace through their hands into the Energy Ball.

4. To conclude, the Collective Energy Ball is ceremoniously released with a Blessing.

I have done this chant many times and it is powerful and shows me that Collective Peace is steadily becoming reality.

Sweeping the Overall Energy Body

This activity is done in couples, where one person uses the Energy Ball to sweep away heavy energy from around the other person's body. This also organizes and Blesses them in light.

This is a non-touch activity, participants choose a partner that they are comfortable with, and then decide who is the giver and the receiver.

1. Participants gaze into each other's eyes and smile, about 50 cm (20 inches) apart.

2. The giving person creates an Energy Ball in the Charging position, and the receiver opens their hands into the Cleansing position, and then places them by their side.

3. The giver places the Energy Ball above the receiver's head.

4. They open their hands very slowly, spreading and guiding the Energy Ball around their head.

5. With fingers spread out, they guide Life Energy from their hands around the receiving person's arms, torso, legs and feet.

6. They move around their entire body using sweeping motions for each area, several times, each time at a slightly faster pace.

7. Then the giving person creates another Energy Ball and places it around the receiving person's body.

8. Again, they gaze into each other's eyes, and notice the effects of the sweeping.

9. They share their experiences for a few minutes and then rinse their hands in water and switch roles.

Energy Ball Hug

Physical hugging makes you feel warm inside and releases oxytocin and serotonin. An Energy Ball Hug connects two or more people's overall energy bodies creating space for them to receive those vital cuddle hormones.

This hug is an intimate experience; therefore, each person chooses for themselves whether to participate and with whom. When given from a distance, visualize hugging the other person.

1. This activity is preceded by the *Sweeping the Overall Energy Body* activity.

2. Both huggers form an Energy Ball in Charging position, and stand facing each other about 1 meter (3 feet) apart.

3. They intensify their Energy Ball by blowing into it, allowing it to expand and fill with abundant Life Energy!

4. They encode it with Friendship and Blessing.

5. One person starts by placing their arms around the other person without touching their body.

6. Once their arms are in place, their partner follows.

7. They notice how it feels to be surrounded and Blessed by the other person and part their overall energy body.

8. They maintain this position for a minute or two.

9. When ready, each partner asks the other if it is appropriate to give the partner a respectful physical hug.

The Energy Ball Hug builds *Friendship Energy*.

Sun Rays Blessing Humanity

This activity extends light Blessings to the surrounding area and its inhabitants. It is called Sun Rays because from above the group looks like a radiating Sun!

1. Form a Collective Energy Ball using the Radiant position.

2. To assist the Collective Energy to come together and intensify, participants acknowledge each other using eye

gazing[41].

3. After a few minutes, the leader asks everyone to simultaneously turn around and, with their hands in the Radiant position, direct Life Energy towards whatever is in front of them, such as the natural landscape, cities, people, animals, or the entire area.

4. Each participant's Energy Ball turns into a Sun Ray of Life Energy and focuses this brightness where it senses energy is needed.

5. Participants say a Blessing silently or out loud.

6. After a few minutes, the leader asks everyone to move in a clockwise direction to the next position.

7. Participants Bless whatever is in front of them with their Sun Ray of Light, and keep moving to a new location, according to the leader's instructions.

---

41   See Eye Gazing, page 78

8. After light energy has been sent out in all directions, everyone turns around and recreates the Collective Energy Ball in the center of the circle.

9. A Blessing is said, and the Collective Energy Ball is ceremoniously lifted upwards and guided by Angelic Friends.

10. Share your experience in a Talking Circle with the Energy Ball[42].

Passing the Energy Ball

This activity helps with group bonding by passing the Energy Ball around the circle. Each person adds their Radiant Blessing into the Ball, and at the end the Collective Ball is released.

1. Each participant forms an individual Energy Ball in the Charging position, and maintains its integrity throughout the ceremony, before and after passing it.

2. The leader begins by encoding the Energy Ball with their Blessing.

---

42   *See Talking Circle with the Energy Ball, page 103*

3. The leader turns to the person on their left (participant A) and very gently passes them the Energy Ball, forming a Couple Energy Ball. After about 20-30 seconds, the leader removes their hands and releases the Energy Ball to participant A.

4. On receiving the Energy Ball, participant A allows it to expand or contract as the Energy Ball wishes, and encodes it with their Blessings.

5. After about 20-30 seconds, participant A passes the Energy Ball to the next person in the circle, participant B. Participant B receives the Energy Ball, infuses it with their Blessing, and then passes it to Participant C.

6. This process continues until the Energy Ball has been passed around the entire circle and returns to the leader.

7. The leader places the Energy Ball into the center of the circle and releases it.

8. The participants turn their hands to the Radiant position and connect to the Collective Ball as it expands and fills the entire center of the circle!

9. The leader says a concluding Blessing:

   Thank you, Creator, for this sacred Energy Ball filled with our bonded spiritual energy. We offer this Blessing as a gift to humanity, so that everyone may awaken and remember the sacredness of Life Energy, and pure light may spread and spread and spread!

10. The group raises up and releases the Energy Ball to the universe in a ceremonious way. The participants then rinse their hands in water.

11. The group shares their experiences in a talking circle with the Energy Ball.

Talking Circle with the Energy Ball

A talking circle expands the vibration that has been created during the Energy Ball for Peace Ceremony. This activity combines the Energy Ball with a Talking Stick. A Talking Stick is an object that defines and honors the person who is speaking in a group setting. It is adopted from the Native American tradition. A leader begins and ends the talking circle.

Remember, thoughtful words are more potent than a long string of words.

- **Activity A** ~ Heart Sharing
- **Activity B** ~ Considering Important Matters

Activity A ~ Heart Sharing

Participants sit in a circle with the Talking Stick in the middle. Participants hold an Energy Ball in one or more of the following hand positions:

- Radiant position ~ holds a sacred, peaceful space and surrounds the speaker in light.
- Nurturing position ~ enables clarification of thoughts, feelings, and centering oneself.

- Charging position ~ builds up the intensity of the collective energy field and feeds the speaker with inspiration.
- Cleansing position ~ enables preparation for speaking and assists with releasing and transformation.

The leader starts by picking up the Talking Stick, and says a Blessing that invites Creator and Angelic Friends to join in the talking circle. The leader then models, by sharing their name, where they live, and one experience they had during the peace ceremony. After completing their presentation, the leader places the Talking Stick in the middle of the circle. Whoever wishes picks it up and expresses themselves. An alternative to this is to pass the Talking Stick around the circle.

When holding the Talking Stick, the speaker shares from their spiritual heart. They focus the energy of all the participants.

To allow the experience of the talking circle to go deeper, the listeners pay careful attention to the speaker, and hold them in the light with the Energy Ball.

Activity B ~ Considering Important Matters

It is vital that important matters be considered in a safe atmosphere. The safe space invites the wisdom of life to flow through the participants and the collective thinking process.

In this activity, the Talking Stick guides the spoken word and the Energy Ball provides the safe space, and brings the collective vibration together. At the end, the Collective Energy Ball is ceremoniously released, honoring and Blessing the important matter.

This activity is divided into rounds. After each round, a summary is written down, to be used in the last round.

The leader explains the procedure and then says a Blessing

inviting Angelic Friends to join and help weave together the collective vibration.

Information Round 1 ~ The leader introduces the important matter. Whomever has specific information picks up the Talking Stick and shares.

Introduction Round 2 ~ The Talking Stick is passed around the circle. Each participant shares their name and how they are connected to the important matter.

Examination Round 3 ~ The Talking Stick is passed around the circle. Each participant shares their passion, experiences, thoughts, insights, and ideas about the important matter.

Brainstorming Round 4 ~ This round stimulates the thinking process. This question helps to begin: "If anything is possible, what would you like to see happen regarding the important matter?" Those that are inspired share by picking up the Talking Stick.

Reality Round 5 ~ Those that plan to do something about the important matter pick up the Talking Stick and state their intention.

Summary Round 6 ~ The Talking Stick is passed around the circle and each participant shares their closing thoughts, with the intention of creating a clear collective vibration.

Blessing and Releasing Round 7 ~ The Talking Stick and the summaries of each round are placed into the center of the circle. All the participants raise their hands into the Radiant position. The leader says a Blessing. The group does the *Toning and the EB* activity[43]. Then the Collective Energy Ball is released with

---

43   *See Toning with the Energy Ball, page 161*

the knowledge that this important matter has been examined and Blessed in a sacred way.

This activity is one of numerous ways to integrate the Energy Ball into group dynamics.

Umbrella of Light ~ Tree Blessing

This ceremony honors and Blesses trees with the gift of a Collective Energy Ball, and develops the connection between humans and trees[44].

1. Begin with the Collective Energy Ball for Peace Ceremony.

2. Form a circle around a tree that you wish to honor.

3. Using the Radiant position, participants connect to and

---

44   *See Blending with a Tree, page 60*

send Life Energy towards the tree.

4. Everyone focuses their attention on the natural beauty and intricacy of the Tree, while sending their light Blessings.

5. The leader says honorary words, such as:

    "Thank you, elder tree, for your presence, you are inspiring! Thank you for the oxygen and the fruits that feed us, your stability and how you stimulate our wisdom! We now honor you with a loving, respectful Collective Energy Ball for Peace."

6. The leader encourages anyone who wishes to say a few words of love and appreciation to honor the awesome creation we call "tree," such as:

    "Thank you, sacred tree, you symbolize so much knowledge, wisdom, strength, flexibility, awesomeness. Thank you for your existence!"

7. Everyone is invited to gently and ceremoniously move towards the tree, finding their unique place around it.

8. Each participant brings their radiate hands closer and closer to the tree without touching it, allowing the tree to absorb the energetic Blessings.

9. Then simultaneously, everyone touches the tree, allowing the Collective Energy with the encoded Blessing to soar up to the top of the tree and radiate out the tree's branches, creating an Umbrella of Light.

10. The tree is then hugged and honored.

11. Participants share their experiences in the *Talking Circle with the Energy Ball*[45].

---

45   *See Talking Circle with the Energy Ball, page 103*

When I do this Ceremony, I see Life Energy from everyone's hands soar up to the top of the tree and out through its branches and leaves. This creates an umbrella of light radiating from the tree to everything beneath it, as well as sending light up, very high up, into the atmosphere. The tree integrates the Blessed human energy with its own energy and radiates out a shower of light, Blessing our world!

When we are under a tree which has been Blessed by the Collective Energy Ball, we are charged and enveloped in the tree's umbrella of light and can feel as large as the tree!

Trees bring spiritual Blessing to human beings. Somehow, tree energy and human energy blend together and combine, creating wisdom and clear thinking.

You can do this activity alone as a harmonizing and nature Blessing experience, by walking around the tree several times with your hands in the Radiant position.

Collective Blessing of Food

Prior to a collective meal, Blessing the food provides a wonderful opportunity to imbue the food everyone is about to ingest with Life Energy. This Blessing assists in building group cohesiveness and sends peaceful, healing vibrations to our world. It complements and can be added to religious food prayers.

1. The leader reads to the group the Blessing Food activity[46].

2. The participants form a circle around the food, cooks, servers, farmers, delivery people and anyone else who helped bring the meal to them.

3. The leader guides the participants through the phases of forming of an Energy Ball.

---

46 *See Blessing Food, page 45.*

4. Everyone takes a moment of silence and connects to their Energy Ball and their inner peace. They are asked to take notice and appreciate their appetite and this opportunity to nourish their body.

5. The leader asks the participants to turn their hands into the Radiant position, creating a Collective Energy Ball that surrounds the food and the people in the center of the circle.

6. A Blessing is said, use this one or create one of your own:

   Thank you, Creator, for the food that is before us and its intended nourishment to our bodies and souls. Thank you for the people who brought it to us, prepared and will serve it. As we partake in the meal, we do so in honor of this abundant amazing Earth upon which we live, and this sacred spiritual reality! Thank you for this gift!

7. At the end of the Blessing, participants raise their hands and release the Energy Ball in thankfulness for the forthcoming nourishment!

8. Participants wash their hands before the meal.

Collective Dancing

Collective dancing with the Energy Ball opens a doorway for dynamic vibrational interaction, especially when joy is brought into the dance.

There are unique ways to dance together with the Energy Ball. Explore and play around with different music and body movements. The variations are endless.

For existing groups, these activities improve relationships. The group members have an opportunity to interact creatively and step out of their usual roles, developing an atmosphere for the group to bond as a team.

- **Activity A** ~ Dancers Meet
- **Activity B** ~ Building Group Energy
- **Activity C** ~ Pulse of Energy
- **Activity D** ~ Sacred Dancing Space
- **Activity E** ~ Passing the Happy Dancing Energy Ball
- **Activity F** ~ Acknowledging Each Other
- **Activity** G ~ Heartdance

Activity A ~ Dancers Meet

1. The leader puts on gentle music and guides the group in the *Energy Ball Dance Ceremony* activity[47].

2. Two dancers blend their Energy Balls together to form a Couple Dancing Energy Ball.

3. Within the couple, one person leads, moving the Energy Ball in diverse directions with their partner following, sensing the flexibility of the Energy Ball. The couple changes who leads often.

4. The person following pays careful attention to their partner's movements, and maintains the integrity of the Couple Energy Ball.

5. The couple moves their arms gently, so as not lose the Couple Energy Ball. The couple's feet, hips, bodies and heads dance to the rhythm of the music.

6. As the Energy Ball builds up in intensity, the dancers increase the distance between them, stretching and expanding into a giant Energy Ball. Sometimes the dancers enjoyably follow the expansion until they reach the walls!

---

47   See *Energy Ball Dance Ceremony, page 196*

7. At a certain point, the Energy Ball begins to contract, and the dancers follow by coming closer together.

8. The vibrating Energy Ball gently guides the dancers on a journey to the rhythm of the music.

9. The couples switch partners whenever they wish. This provides dancers an opportunity to meet each other, and experience dancing with the Energy Ball in a different and unique way.

Activity B ~ Building Group Energy

1. Play music with a medium rhythm.

2. Two couples join together to form groups of four dancers. Here the energy is more flexible, playful, and expansive.

3. The Energy Ball is held in the center of them, and bounces to the rhythm of the music.

4. One person leads the group with creative movements, and the others playfully follow along.

5. Notice that a surge of dance energy bubbles up from within and guides the Collective Dancing Energy Ball.

6. Switch the leader often, giving everyone who wishes an opportunity to guide the group dance with the Energy Ball.

7. Join with other groups, and create larger and more dynamic dancing circles.

Activity C ~ Pulse of Energy

1. The leader invites all the dancers into one circle.

2. Rhythmic music is put on and participants dance in place with their Energy Ball, and sing along with the song.

3. The dancers raise their hands in the Radiant position, forming a Collective Energy Ball in the center of the circle.

4. They push their hands in and out, pumping the Collective Energy Ball.

5. On the leader's signal, the entire circle simultaneously dances towards the center of the circle with their hands in the Radiant position, thereby pushing and condensing the Collective Energy Ball into a compact mass of Life Energy filled with the group's dancing vibration.

6. There is a certain point where the Collective Energy Ball sufficiently compacts and pushes the group outwards, recreating the larger circle.

7. Once again, the group dances inwards, pushing the Energy Ball, and waits until the intensity of the ball pushes them out again.

8. They gracefully follow this inward and outward motion to the rhythm of the music. This creates a wave of energy.

9. Conclude with enthusiastically jumping up and releasing the Collective Energy Ball with excitement and joy!

Activity D ~ Sacred Dancing Space

1. Dancers stand in a circle with the hands in the Radiant position, creating a safe space in the middle of the circle to dance.

2. One person enters the center of the circle and dances with their Energy Ball in their unique way. Everyone else follows their movements. For larger groups 2-5 people are in the center.

3. Those in the circle copy the movement of the person in the

center's Energy Ball if they wish.

4. The person (people) in the middle changes often, allowing everyone who wishes to express their unique dance.

Inspired dancers may jump in and join the person in the center. This sometimes causes the entire group to jump into the center and form an Ecstatic Collective Dancing Energy Ball!

Activity E ~ Passing the Happy Dancing Energy Ball

1. Create a sacred dancing space as described in the previous activity.

2. The leader steps into the center of the circle and dances with their Energy Ball to a happy song, exaggerating certain movements, seeking to receive a laugh.

3. After a half a minute or less, the leader goes to another dancer and gives them the Energy Ball charged with their happiness.

4. They receive the charged Energy Ball and then dance around the circle adding their unique flavor of joy.

5. Then they find another person in the circle and pass the Happy Energy Ball to them.

6. This goes on until all the Dancers have added their Joy, and enthusiasm for Life into the Energy Ball!

7. The group recreates the circle with the Happy Dancing Energy Ball in the center.

8. Then everyone turns to their left and the Leader begins an Energy Ball Line Dance, going around the dance floor spreading their Collective Joy!

Activity F ~ Acknowledging Each Other

1. Form two circles, one within the other, with the inner circle facing the outer circle. Throughout the entire dance, the circles move in opposite directions at a consistent very slow speed.

2. The participants hold their hands in the Radiant position and, look into the eyes of the person opposite them in the other circle while dancing to the music with the Energy Ball.

3. Dancers slowly but constantly move so the connection with each person is for a short time.

4. The circle keeps going until everyone has connected and danced with everyone else.

5. Then groups of 3-5 people continue dancing with the Collective Energy Ball.

These two circles can be: women ~ men, guest ~ regulars, children ~ adults, or other combinations.

Activity G ~ Heartdance

During the Heartdance, two dancers give and receive heart energy with each other.

Use gentle music and move your arms and body smoothly.

This is an intimate dance. Everyone is asked to find a partner that they are comfortable with. They decide who will start as the giver and who will be the receiver.

For romantic couples, this activity deepens your relationship.

The leader demonstrates with their partner:

1. Both the giver and receiver hold an Energy Ball in the in front of their heart in the Charging position. They sway their bodies to the music and connect to their inner strengthen.

2. Each one says a Blessing of appreciation, love and respect for their partner, encoding the Energy Ball.

3. While dancing, the giver takes a deep breath, and does two things at the same time:

    • Blows Life Energy into the Energy Ball.

    • Slowly, gracefully moves their hands outwards into the Radiant position with their hands facing their partner's heart, about 20 cm (8 inches) away from them.

4. The receiver moves their hands from the Charging position, with their arms wide open and stretched out in front of them. They guide the Heart Energy Ball inwards towards their physical heart, with a few sweeping motions of the hands.

5. After receiving the Heart Energy Ball, they say "Thank you!" They take a deep breath and extend the Heart Energy Ball back to their partner.

6. Their Partner stretches out their arms and receives the heart energy, and then returns it. They continue with giving and receiving Heart Energy for as long as they wish.

7. Participants can stay with one partner the entire dance, or switch partners.

Story ~ The College of Respect

A young girl named Ora approached the checkout counter to pay for her supplies. With a nasty look, the clerk rudely threw the change back at her. It was like a dagger in her pure heart and she began to cry. The clerk and his friends made fun of her and laughed.

Ora ran home to tell her Mom what happened. Her Mom responded, saying "Some people never learned to be respectful. Disrespect has wounded and filled them up with impurity. They should not be taken to heart. They simply need your compassion and light Blessings."

Then she taught Ora the Energy Ball to maintain her pure, lovely spirit and how to use it to dissolve impure vibrations. Her Mom continued sharing with Ora the meaning of respect: *Respect is an inner power, it is a way of thinking and living. Unfortunately, many people have lost their connection to respect, and you met some of them today.*

Smile at people; look them in the eyes. Don't impose yourself. Wait your turn to speak, listen to what someone is saying, and discuss what they say. Don't argue with them. Respect is honoring, and it comes from your heart.

From that moment on Ora payed attention to how respectful or disrespectful people behaved. She noticed that many people carried the spirit of respect inside of them, and knew how to express it. She felt good being around these people. Other people seemed to be disrespectful for no reasons whatsoever. Sometimes, she would inquire why and discovered they were **unaware** that their actions and words were disrespectful!! They were just doing what everyone else does. Rapidly her passion for spreading the consciousness of Respect grew into her life's calling!

After graduating high school, Ora decided to major in Respect at college. To her astonishment, there were no schools ready to teach respect as a major area of study. Eventually, Ora found a small alternative college that allowed her to major in *Promoting the Consciousness of Respect*. She created her own curriculum, immersed herself in the *World of Respect*, focusing on the reasons why individuals and societies were respectful and disrespectful.

Ora began by taking surveys, inquiring about awareness of respectful and disrespectful attitudes and actions in their community. She asked about their respect training and how respectful attitudes were shared between their friends and within their family.

With this information, she created an evaluation sheet, allowing her to analyze the levels of respect and disrespect present in individuals and the community. She then created a few tools to guide individuals and communities out of disrespect:

- A booklet called "Choose Respect". The basics about individual and collective Respect.
- The "Respect Ceremony", based on the Energy Ball Ora learned from her Mom as a child.

After Ora graduated from college, she sought out financial backing. Eventually, one wealthy woman recognized her potential and visited Ora. Following their first bonding conversation, they instantly became life-long friends and she jumped into Ora's life! She was not only the benefactor, also an advisor and a vital member of the Respect Team!

They invited all the respectful people they knew to a Respect Ceremony. It was an amazing success, drawing vibrant people from all over the Planet Earth!

At the gathering, a Respect Team was formed. Some of the

team were from Spiritual Peace groups in Israel and Palestine and they insisted that Ora and her Respect Team bring The Spirit of Respect to their problematic region.

Ora and the Respect Team accepted.

They discussed what would be the best approach for them to introduce the Spirit of Respect, and decided to have a series of at least 20 Respect Ceremonies in strategic locations around Israel and Palestine. There they would distribute the booklet "Choose Respect".

The gatherings focused on being creative with the concept of Respect. They considered how each one can influence their community with their words and actions, thereby creating a Respectful society. These gatherings were fun, creative, and very exciting!

Some of the topics they considered were respectfully living with your neighbors, respecting yourself, respecting Planet Earth, and respecting food and water.

After this series of events, Ora and her benefactor opened a training school on the Sea of Galilee, which quickly turned into the "The College of Respect".

The College grew in many directions:

1. Instructing individuals and teachers in the:
   - Respect Method
   - Art of Communicating the Spirit of Respect
   - Respect Ceremony

2. The College included a Respect Research Department, to expose common disrespectful attitudes that are present in society, but unrecognized, and to provide creative solutions to transform these communities into Respectful places to live.

3. It organized learning through Respect Projects, a few examples:

- "Driving with Respect" program: Teaching automobile drivers how to create safer roads. This was enormously successful, and led to Respect lessons becoming required in order to maintain a driver's license in Israel, and several other countries.

- Respecting the Natural World: Cleaning up and repairing natural areas; and instructing people on how to Respect all aspects of nature.

- Television and radio station were taught how to play respectful music and talk shows focused on educating people how to be respectful.

- Musicians were guided to create respectful songs that inspire people to be wiser.

The College of Respect's reputation began to spread into the educational facilities throughout the world. Their work was translated into many languages, leading to a global consciousness of Respect.

Respect became natural, resulting in happier and healthier children, parents, families, teachers and school workers.

Many could actually see the infusion of Respect as a translucent light purple haze filling the atmosphere, spreading to every part of the globe.

At this point fewer and fewer people wished to spoil this growing respectful atmosphere, evidence that the Collective consciousness to Respect was overtaking Planet Earth.

This meant that they succeeded, and there was no longer a need for The College of Respect. So, they shut the doors and went on a long and joyful vacation!!

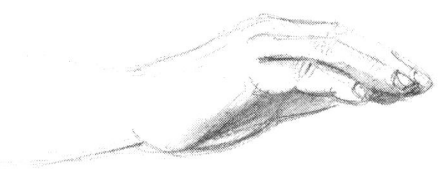

Section 4:
Going Deeper

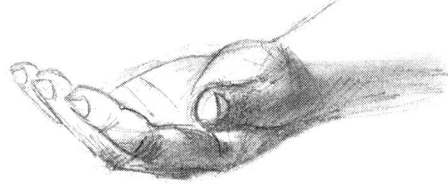

Chapter 11: Nuances

I use words and phrases slightly differently than the common usage. This chapter explains a few of them.

- Life Energy
- Pure Life Energy
- Impure Energy
- Light
- Overall Energy Body
- Blessing
- Ray of Light
- Sacred Space
- Invisible World

Life Energy

Life Energy is a continuous gift from Creator as it flows through and animates our body. This vital essence enlivens and rejuvenates our cells. It is often known as the Essence of Life.

Life Energy flows in a current and appears to me to be part of Sunlight. It nurtures us with its etheric food, rejuvenating us!

We have the ability to control and guide the amount and quality of our Life Energy moving through our body with the Energy Ball.

When we encourage a strong current of life to flow through our body, we become radiant, strong, vibrant, filled with health and vigor.

Some people disrespect the Current of Life, resulting in the lack of desire to be actively alive, leading to weakness and illness.

Life Energy can be felt in the hands and encoded with intention.

Pure Life Energy

Pure Life Energy is experienced as crystal clear flowing water, and has the vibration of innocence. It is common to identify this very, very clean essence around a newborn baby, genuine love and pristine Nature. It is often seen around Sunrise and Sunset time as waves of light.

People with Pure Life Energy are drawn to each other and nurture one another. When they bond together as a team, their Light influence greatly increases.

I love to be around Pure Life Energy. I feel renewed, enlivened and sense anything is possible!

Impure Energy

It is very, very sad for me to say to you that Planet Earth's atmosphere is energetically polluted with what I call Impure Energy. This is a very large topic, and to begin to understand Impure Energy, consider these thoughts:

- Impure Energy is fascinating in its ingenuity to create chaos.

- With Impure Energy, I am constantly learning what not to do.

- Impure Energy is tricky and has numerous ways of becoming entangled into a person's life experiences.

- Evidence of Impure Energy's presence is its draining, pulling, unpleasant affect, and sometimes it has a foul odor.

- When a person allows Impure Energy to latch onto them, their personality changes, and they become needy.

- Too much interaction with Impure Energy makes a person think in an impure way, resulting in a weak and complicated life experience.

- People attract Impure Energy with a taking attitude, cussing, nasty unkind words and actions.

- It is wise to avoid situations where impure vibrations are created and collect.

The Energy Ball easily neutralizes Impure Energy's chaotic vibrations by introducing a pure Energetic flow of fresh Life Energy. This often happens without our conscious awareness, we simply know that when we form an Energy Ball we feel better and lighter.

When Impure Energy has a grip on a person, they can remove it by doing the Self-Blessing activity daily for a few weeks[48].

For really stuck Impure Energy, I use Spiritual Guidance, Somatic Experiencing ®[49] and Attunement[50].

Light

Our Sun radiates out a continuous wave that nourishes everything it touches with its essence. This Light Energy is then absorbed, transformed and the resulting radiance we experience as "Light".

Light comes out of every part of Creation: people, animals, rocks, vegetation... Each one has it's own unique Light Code, which can be sensed with our Perceptive ability and the Energy Ball.

Learning the Language of Light allows us to more easily participate and enjoy our life experience on Planet Earth.

---

48   See Self-Blessings, page 52
49   See Somatic Experiencing®, page 207
50   See Attunement, page 207

Overall Energy Body

I call the Light Energy that emanates from the physical body the *Overall Energy Body*. It consists of Life Energy that is constantly flowing from every part of the body. It is often called the "Aura" and is described as having energetic layers called *subtle bodies*.

The size and the quality of the Overall Energy Body is constantly changing. It is different for each person, depending on what they are experiencing in the moment, their location on Planet Earth, the people they are with, their mood......

To guide or adjust my Overall Energy Body, I use the Energy Ball and my intent. I keep my Overall Energy Body very flexible and about a meter away from my body. This makes me ready for incoming vibrations from the outside environment.

When I am in a pure, safe space, my Overall Energy Body expands and I feel like a giant! This feels very natural and brings me a great deal of pleasure!

When I am in a crowded or impure location, I may choose to bring my Overall Energy Body in very close to my physical body to avoid the chaotic vibrations.

Having control over our Overall Energy Body takes intuition, perception, intention and being connected to our internal Life Energy flow. The Energy Ball makes it simpler[51]!

Blessing

When words are said in a nurturing manner, the vibration that comes out is a Blessing. Nurturing words directed into the Energy Ball charge the contained Life Energy with sacredness. I call this Encoding the Energy Ball with Blessing[52].

---

51   See *Adjusting your Overall Energy Body*, page 55.
52   See *Encoding the Energy Ball with Blessing*, page 38

During the individual or Collective Ceremony, Blessings are sent out when the Energy Ball is released into the atmosphere.

- Energetic Blessings assist in maintaining a sacred atmosphere on Planet Earth. Every Blessing is important and vital!

- The quality of Energy that is encoded into the Energy Ball depends upon the vibration of the individuals in the group and how they come together as a team.

- Powerful Energetic Blessings are created when two or more Peace People lovingly, joyfully and respectfully come together and encode the Collective Energy Ball, creating a Peace Team!

Ray of Light

A Ray of Light is created when Life Energy is focused into a beam. It provides an intensified burst of Life Energy to wherever it is directed. This focused Light has a very specific use and can be guided to nurture[53].

- When directed inside the body, it dissolves frozen and stuck vibrations.

- It is used to perceive the purity of Life Energy.

- It enhances our ability to touch the essence of Nature.

- It is used to neutralize Energetic pollution from Planet Earth.

- *Because the Ray of Light is powerful, before sending it to another person ask their permission[54].*

---

53   *See Ray of Light Position, page 160*
54   *See Gifting the Energy Ball, page 168.*

Sacred Space

When Pure Life Energy flows into the same location on a consistent basis a Sacred Space is created.

A Sacred Space is a clean and clear environment, it feels like you and everything around you are in the Flow of Life Energy with unlimited potential! When a person creates Energy Balls often, they live in and carry around Sacred Space, which leads them into amazing experiences!

Angels love to come to a Sacred Space, and enjoy being with people who shine their Light!

The Energy Ball for Peace Ceremony is a simple way to experience and create Collective Sacred Space!

Invisible World

When growing up I noticed that there was a lot going on that could not be visually seen. I enjoyed these experiences and interactions and began to call this reality the Invisible World. Then I learned that I was actually connecting to the Spiritual World, and that this unseen reality has many, many aspects to it, with an enormous amount to teach me!

It is a great adventure to have the Invisible ~ Spiritual World adjacent to our physical reality and available for interaction!

Learning how to relate to the Invisible World and its many, many parts is an art!

With the Energy Ball, we:

- Create a connection to Invisible World
- Receive Spiritual Information
- Help clarify the Invisible World's vibrations
- Are reminded of our Angelic Nature

Clear communication and interaction with the Invisible World is a vital ingredient to living a happy, healthy life on Planet Earth.

This guidebook is filled with ways to integrate and nourish the relationship between the Invisible World and present-day realities.

Chapter 12: Philosophy

The Energy Ball stimulates the desire to think and live as an Energetically alive Human Being!

- The Language of Light Energy
- Shining Being of Light
- Being in the Flow of Life!
- Spirit of Peace
- Spiritual Sight

The Language of Light Energy

One day I realized that Light Energy was speaking to me. It was an instinctive understanding that made me curious and excited! As the years went on, I understood that Light has consistency in its numerous vibrational patterns, and used my intuition to help me learn the meaning of these unique sensations.

In the early 1970's, I learned to guide Light Energy with my hands into another person's body without touching them, in an Energetic Balancing Ceremony called Attunement[55]. Consciously sending and receiving Life Energy opened up a whole world for me.

Now I could receive and send Light information: Wow!

Eventually, I saw that every part of Nature has a meaning and can be understood by learning its unique vibrational code. I then applied this to the physical body and realized that Light has a Language!

Learning the Language of Light Energy, aids in the understanding and participating with the Essence of Life.

---

55   *See Attunement, page 207*

Light Energy:

- Communicates all the time, speaking with pulses, vibrations and sensations. These are Light Energy's letters and words. Its stories are images, thoughts and feelings.
- Speaks very subtly, and therefore often goes unnoticed.
- Is always in motion, constantly giving and receiving information between the physical reality and the Invisible World.

The Energy Ball makes it easier to perceive Life's messages.

Shining Being of Light

Have you ever seen a person so bright and full of Life that your face lights up just by looking at them? They are what I call a "Shining Being of Light" or a "Walking Energy Ball". Their Overall Energy Body radiates like our Sun!

- Everyone is a "Being of Light", but not everyone shines!
- When a person chooses to shine their Light brightly, they increase the amount and quality of Life Energy that circulates and comes out of their body. They become radiant!
- When the Being of Light is not paid attention to, the flow of Life Energy through the body greatly diminishes. This creates an unhealthy internal atmosphere in and around the person, resulting in emotional, mental and physical problems.
- Shining Beings of Light are the eyes of Creator, and assist in overseeing humanity!

The Energy Ball for Peace Ceremony makes it easy for Shining Beings of Light to come together and send out a burst of Light Energy that is a magnificent and beautiful reflection of Creator. I call us Collective Human Angels and Peace Teams!

Being in the Flow of Life!

When I am walking in Nature, after a short time, I arrive at an automatic pace. My body naturally goes step by step, my senses take in creation, and I easily receive each new life experience, flowing with Life.

Each person flows with the current of life in their own unique way. Often it is experienced through routine daily chores.

- The physical sensation of flowing with life is feels lighter, flexible, happier, healthier, and wiser.

- Life Energy constantly flows in and around all the body systems. It moves, changes, increases and decreases, as required.

- The natural state of the Energetic body is to flow with the current of Life Energy.

- A clear flow of Life Energy naturally melts impure, unclean and distorted Energy so that we may live a purer and clearer life.

- Consciously being in the flow of life allows us to guide our life experience.

Spirit of Peace

Peace exists, but not enough people are paying attention! I often make this statement at Peace gatherings. Then I add, Peace is an atmosphere, it is everywhere, sometimes hidden and hard to find; sometimes out in the open and easy to experience. Always, Peace, is creating a Sacred Space with its tranquil vibration.

The Energy Ball gives us a way to pay attention to the Spirit of Peace and to easily send Blessings and Prayers filled with Peaceful vibrations!

When we are guided by the Spirit of Peace, something happens inside of us; we are internally stimulated and become Vibrant, Joyful, Hopeful and Radiant! This is evidence that the Spirit of Peace is alive inside. With consistency, the Spirit of Peace transforms our life and we turn into a Peace Person. When two or more Peace People come together they form a Peace Team!

Spiritual Sight

Spiritual Sight is a very natural and wonderful gift from Creator! It is the experience of peering into and perceiving the invisible world.

These are a few of the many names associated with Spiritual Sight: clairvoyance, intuition, Spiritual perception, mind reading, psychic ability, telepathy, ESP, divination, prophecy, insight......

Developing Spiritual Sight into a perceptive tool is an exciting personal journey[56].

A few thoughts:

- Looking between your hands and into the Energy Ball stimulates and develops your perceptive ability.

- Watching Sunrises and Sunsets with the Energy Ball feeds and stimulates your perceptive abilities.

- Spiritual Sight goes through stages of development throughout a person's lifetime.

- Some people have a greater capacity to utilize their Spiritual Sight then others. This depends upon their life experiences and their family history of using Spiritual Sight.

---

56   *See Spiritual Sight Development, page 163*

- Each person uses their Spiritual Sight in a unique way.

- We learn how to use our Spiritual Sight by noticing with how much purity other people use their Spiritual Sight.

- When Spiritual Sight is ignored, it atrophies, causing stuck emotions and complicated thoughts.

- When Spiritual Sight becomes damaged, consistent use with the Energy Ball helps it to repair.

- Clear Spiritual Sight helps us avoid encounters with impure vibrations.

- Spiritual Sight can be blocked and cleared from the blockage with the Energy Ball.

Some of what can be perceived in the Invisible World:

- Pure Beautiful, Light Energy
- Energetic flow of Angels
- Damaged, confused and manipulated vibrations
- Essence of Life
- Sunlight and Starlight
- Creator's vastness!

Story ~ The Billionaire and the Energy Ball for Peace Ceremony

For most of my life, I have envisioned and philosophized about World Peace, especially if money was abundant.

This is one of my ideas in the form of a story:

One day a Billionaire was given a new book by her secretary; "The Energy Ball for Peace Ceremony: Personal Health and Global Blessing", and simply introduced it as "I believe that this is the new direction for humanity".

When the Billionaire read the book she laughed, as she had often made Energy Balls, and had wondered how humanity could harness this sacred power.

For the past several years, the Billionaire and her associates had been assisting with many humanitarian projects, but felt that they were not doing nearly enough. They were constantly brainstorming, and sincerely wanted to find a way to assist human beings to become a Peaceful Species on Planet Earth!

Immediately, she contacted the author and arranged a meeting.

Together they explored the World of the Energy Ball, and the numerous ways in which it has the ability to help humanity.

The outcome of their time together was a Humanitarian Project called **"The Energy Ball for World Harmony"**.

The Billionaire then invited her colleagues to a meeting so that she could encourage them to become active participants, not only with their money, but also with their time, wisdom, name and influence!

In her speech to them, she emphasized that to strengthen World Harmony requires teamwork, and with the Energy Ball for Peace Ceremony we can easily form teams and guide Humanity into becoming a more Peaceful, respectful, loving species on

Planet Earth!!

Here are a few of their intended projects:

- Translate and distribute this guidebook, "Energy Ball for Peace Ceremony" to every country on Planet Earth.

- Train Energy Ball for Peace Ceremony leaders.

- Adapt the Energy Ball for Peace Ceremony to be used in different settings, cultures and audiences.

- Develop supportive teams of Peace Cheerleaders to travel to every part of the globe conducting Collective Energy Ball for Peace Ceremonies and teaching its many uses.

- Develop Live Streaming Collective Energy Ball for Peace Ceremonies throughout the world.

- Create a series of movies and television programs that educate and encourage using the Energy Ball on a daily basis for health, personal growth, and development, and to assist with World Blessing.

- Create Energy Ball Research/Therapy Centers in strategic locations around the globe. These centers will prove the benefits and uses of the Energy Ball in overcoming problems and disease, while providing service to anyone who needs assistance.

- Introduce the Energy Ball into learning institutions, and intertwine it with the current curriculum, creating an atmosphere for exciting learning.

- Invite hospital emergency rooms to have Energy Ball Therapists in their waiting rooms.

- Create Alternative Emergency rooms and a hospital for Spiritual and psychological care.

- Train individuals and groups in using the Energy Ball for overcoming collective trauma and conflict.

- Develop a world effort to clean up environmental pollution and to teach recycling, using the Energy Ball for Peace Ceremony to inspire people to enthusiastically participate.

- Teach politicians and government officials to utilize the Energy Ball in creating an atmosphere for making correct decisions.

- To push forward the consciousness of Peace, and resolve collective problems; set up a large network of Energy Ball for Peace and Conflict Resolution Centers on each side of the problematic area; and conduct daily Peace Ceremonies.

- Create a fleet of Energy Ball for Peace ships that sail from port to port around the globe, teaching the Energy Ball, and helping in every way they can to Create Peace.

I can only imagine what it would be like for a Billionaire to take on The Energy Ball for Peace Ceremony Vision.......

But regardless of money, we can feed World Peace by:

- Creating Energy Balls often, and encoding them with Blessings of Peace.

- Creating Collective Energy Ball for Peace Ceremonies.

- Talking about the Energy Ball, and teaching others how to form an Energy Ball.

- Envisioning Humanity living on Planet Earth in a Peaceful, Loving, Respectful way!

- Participate often in the Ceremony to Bless Humanity[57] and the Ceremony to Hug Planet Earth[58] often.

---

57 See Ceremony to Bless Humanity, page 184
58 See Ceremony to Hug Planet Earth, page 182

Chapter 13
Creator and Angelic Friends

Creator and our Angelic Friends love to come whenever someone makes an Energy Ball. It is a signal that says, "this human being is an available open channel."

The philosophy and activities in this chapter assist in using the Energy Ball to connect to Creator and your Angelic Friends.

- Creator
- Angelic Friends
- Human Angel
- Collective Human Angels
- Angels and the Energy Ball for Peace Ceremony
- Group Blessing to Welcome Creator and Angels
- Connecting to Creator with the Energy Ball
- Connecting to Angels with the Energy Ball
- Calling in Angels with the Energy Ball
- More About Angels
- More About Creator
- Story ~ The First Energy Ball

Creator

I look at Creator as the source of the *Essence of Life*, who somehow took matter, fed it with Life Energy, and created this magnificent creation.

Human beings are privileged to play the vital role of bringing Creator's Essence onto Planet Earth. When we form an Energy Ball, we take the first step of consciously preparing a space to create with Life Energy.

I realized long ago, that when I genuinely thank, appreciate and give my love to Creator, a burst of Life Energy moves between me and Creator. When I consciously express thankfulness, and form an Energy Ball at the same time, a potent harmonious vibration is created! The quantity of Light Energy flowing through my body increases, and space is created inside of me. Therefore, I am available to receive and contain even more Life Energy from Creator.

This is what I call a *Connected* Human Being, a person who is enhancing *Creator's Creation*!

- Our Creator smiles and encourages us each time we form an Energy Ball.

- In the Energy Ball for Peace Ceremony we use Blessings of thankfulness, appreciation and love to invite Creator and Creator's assistants, Angels, to participate. When the Ceremony is experienced on a regular basis, a firm connection is developed between Creator and each Human Being participating.

- Angels work with Creator to enliven human experience, and greatly increase the amount and quality of Life Energy present.

- Connecting to Creator and Angels is a very personal experience. Each Human Being is responsible to feed and nurture their connection for themselves.

- People who love Creator are excellent examples and guides and make great friends! It is enormously beneficial to have loving people in our life!

- Creator and Angels have been endlessly studied and philosophized. This has made the words "creator and angel" to have many, many meanings, related concepts, and interpretations, resulting in an enormous amount of confusion and imagination about them.

- This guidebook is a way to clarify, connect to, and learn from Creator and our Angelic Friends.

- If you do not believe in Creator and Angels, I invite you to release your preconceived thoughts about them, and flow with the Energy Ball activities. After a while, you will have your own proof.

Angelic Friends

Creator sparked the Essence of Life creating Angelic Presence, which spread into all matter. The result in what we call Creation. Every aspect of *Creation* has its own unique type of Angelic Presence, some very conscious, some less conscious.

Since there are so many types of Angelic Presence, and to make it simpler for me to understand, I say that there are Angels in human form and many, many types and categories of Etheric Angels. Some of these Etheric Angels are my *Angelic Friends*.

I first realized that I had Angelic Friends when I was young, but did not acknowledge them as Angels. I simply called them *my friends without physical bodies*.

There were many occasions when Etheric Angels approached me around museums and libraries, guiding me to books, artwork and people that were perfect for my spiritual development at that moment.

Eventually, I understood that I was not the only one who had these types of experiences. I realized that Etheric Angels are the Essence of Life, without a physical form, and very enjoyable to have in my life! I found out that they intensify Spiritual Light, and bring a very strong atmosphere of assurance, joy and love.

Now I call them my Angelic Friends, and see them as cheerleaders, guiding humanity towards the Light!

Our Angelic Friends:

- Exist in a semi-visible dimension, and easily travel in the Light
- Actively watch and guide humans
- Are drawn to Pure Energy, genuine prayer, and Blessings that comes from the heart
- Are not always recognized as Angels
- Remind humans that we are the pure Essence of Life ~ Angels in human form
- Are filled with vigor and information
- Provide a safe, resilient, happy experience
- Are repelled when people fight and are arrogant; then they help from a distance
- Like to be lovingly invited to join into an activity

Everyone has Angelic Friends!

The Energy Ball creates a Sacred Space that attracts Angels.

When I sense Angelic Presence, I say "Thank You for coming! Please join me in spreading Light Blessings!!"

Human Angel

Every human being is the Essence of Life in a physical body, and an Angel in human form. I believe that it is a privilege to have a physical body and to be on Planet Earth!

A conscious Human Angel interacts with the Invisible World, is spiritually responsible, and is a creative Human Being. We are inspired people who bring hope, inspiration, and visions for humanity living on Planet Earth Peacefully! In this guidebook,

I call Human Angels *Peace People*.

An unconscious Human Angel uses very little of its full potential, and often causes problems with its actions and words.

Collective Human Angels

Collective Human Angels are two or more Human Angels who merge and harmonize together as a Light Team, with the intention of sharing their Collective Blessing. Evidence of Collective Human Angels is that they send out potent Light, truly enjoy being together and time stands still for them!

The Energy Ball for Peace Ceremony brings Human Angels together, and changes ordinary groups of human beings into a Collective of Human Angels, also called Peace Teams. When Collective Human Angels come together on a consistent basis, they develop a following of Angelic Friends. Often multitudes of Angelic Friends set up an etheric living room over the Sacred Space where Human Angels gather.

Angels and the Energy Ball for Peace Ceremony

Angels are an important part of the Peace Ceremony:

- They are honored guests.
- They bring abundant sparkly Light Energy with them.
- They are excited caretakers of the Blessings, as they accompany and guide the Energy Ball on its journey.

Group Blessing to Welcome Creator and Angels

All Blessings of connecting and communication with Creator and Angels are welcome during the Energy Ball for Peace Ceremony. Here is an example of a universal Blessing:

Thank you, Creator and Angelic Friends, for coming

and bringing your Love-Light! We welcome you to participate with us as we radiate our Collective Energy and create a Sacred Space for Life to blossom, so that all of humanity and Planet Earth may be Blessed and enlightened!

Connecting to Creator with the Energy Ball

This activity provides the opportunity to strengthen your connection to Creator.

1. Preparation: Perform the activity *Calming the Emotions*[59].

2. Form an Energy Ball in the Nurturing position.

3. Make a solid connection to yourself through slow and steady breathing, building up internal trust.

4. Say a Blessing such as the following:

    Thank you, Creator, for this present moment in eternity! Thank you for the breath of life and the opportunity to be here! I am ready to create with you on Planet Earth right now!

5. Move your hands to the Light Connection position, and feel yourself in as a Channel of Light.

6. Feel your genuine appreciation for Creator bubbling up inside of you, and again express your thankfulness.

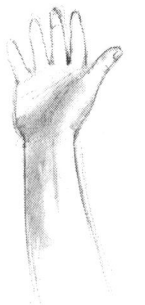 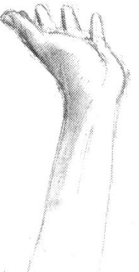

---

59 *See Calming the Emotions, page 176*

7. Notice how the vibration of appreciation is sent through your hands up into the atmosphere.

8. Sense how Creator instantly returns abundant Life Energy to you, filling your body to overflowing and expanding your Overall Energy Body!

9. This is a time to pay careful attention to whatever realizations come to you.

10. Move your hands into the Charging position, and sense how your body feels Peaceful, and that you are connected to Creator. With renewed excitement, you are ready for your next adventure here on Planet Earth! Go for it!

Connecting to Angels with the Energy Ball

There are many levels to connect to our Angelic Friends. Utilizing the Energy Ball allows us to be closer:

1. Form an Energy Ball in the Nurturing position.

2. Say words of Blessing and invitation. Here is one that I often use:

   Greetings my Angelic Friends! It feels wonderful to connect with you, please join me so we can experience Life together! Thank you for coming!

3. Feel yourself surrounded and Blessed by their presence. It feels warm, comfortable and secure.

4. Then say: *I would like to connect closer to you and invite you. Would you like to form an Energy Ball with me?*

5. Instantly, your hands will be drawn in very close towards each other, creating a very tiny and hot Energy Ball with your Angelic Friend. (If this does not happen use the *Spiritual Sight Development* activity.[60])

---

60   *See Spiritual Sight Development, page 163*

6. Put your attention on the Mystical Heaven that descends upon you. Notice that there is a sharp increase in the intensity of the Energy that flows through your hands and body.

7. My experience is that the Energy feels thicker, molten, and carries transformative vibrations. This is evidence that both you and your Angelic Friend have encoded the Energy Ball with your Spiritual Energy.

8. At a certain point, the Energy Ball will start to expand. Allow your hands to move outwards with the sensation. This makes the Energy Ball larger and larger.

9. Stretch your arms to their maximum distance from your body.

10. Blow into the Energy Ball, and quickly spread your fingers, allowing Angelic Energy to surround and Bless your Overall Energy Body!

11. Form another Energy Ball in the Light Connection position, and say a Blessing:

   Thank you, Creator, for this connection to my Angelic Friend. This Blessing is an open invitation for each individual Human Being to acknowledge and connect to their Angelic Friends and to play their part in waking up sleeping humanity. Together we extend our Blessings encoded with loving vibrations!

12. The slowly bring your hands down around your entire body, and touch the ground.

Enjoy your experience of being immersed in Light, and intimately connected to your Angelic Friend!!

Calling in Angels with the Energy Ball

Sometimes, when I am around human beings who function with a very low level of Life Energy, and/or there is environmental pollution, it becomes harder for me to make a connection to my Angelic Friends, so I use the following procedure:

1. I form an Energy Ball in the Nurturing position, and take a few minutes focusing and clearing myself.

2. I move my hands into the Charging position, and envision sending up a thin antenna of Light, high into the atmosphere, way beyond human interference.

3. Then I open up a channel to my Angelic Friends with a Blessings, and invite them to join me: *Hello my Angelic Friends, there is interference here on Earth and I would love to connect to you. Please come join me and connect.*

4. Once I feel the connection, the thin antennae of Light becomes wider and spreads, creating a space charged with Angelic presence.

5. Then I invite them to communicate with me, using inviting words of trust and appreciation. The evidence of this connection is that my Overall Energy Body becomes organized, feels purer and shines. It feels like being nurtured spiritually, and at the same time being fed with ancient wisdom.

6. When you are ready, spread your arms and the Energy Ball as far as you can reach, expanding your Overall Energy Body, and creating a larger Sacred Space.

7. Notice that your Angelic Friends stay with you and Guide you in your Life!

What happens is this: the Energy Ball helps to melt away the chaotic vibrations that is in the atmosphere. Once the atmosphere is clear, it is easier for Angels to communicate with us.

More about Angels

- Sense how Angelic Energy affects the intensity and size of the Energy Ball.

- Angels are always present. Paying attention to them is a conscious choice!

- Each Angel has a very unique Energetic Essence. Notice whether their presence and quality is familiar, or reminds you of someone, or some experience.

- Angels love to participate with you and experience human Life! They love invitations such as *"Welcome, let's form an Energy Ball together and Radiate out our Light!"*

- Angels are attracted by Pure Energy, Love, and a giving attitude.

- Angels are repelled by a needy attitude and impure vibrations.

- As we flow with Angelic Energy, we understand and can share their wisdom.

- When we make a solid connection with Angels, our connection with Creator becomes consistent.

- I do not ask my Angelic Friends for anything, because they already know how to help. They simply need our awareness and an invitation to participate. Then they stimulate us in just the right way!!

More about Creator

To identify with Creator is knowing the sensation of Creator inside of our body. Our breathing, heartbeat, and body rhythms constantly remind us of the magnificence of Creator. When we identify with Creator, our identity shifts so that we actually are an active part of Creator, and therefore connected with all of

Creation. Everything we do and say is an expression of Creator. We therefore are Creator's way to express on Planet Earth.

Story ~ The First Energy Ball

After men and women were just created, God said, "Put your hands very close together, almost touching, and notice what happens."

Men and women did so, and their eyes lit up!

God then said, "What you feel between your hands is Life Energy. Now bend your fingers, and form this Energy into a Ball. Pay careful attention to it. Therein is everything you need to know about living a healthy, vibrant Spiritual Life on this lush Planet!"

From that moment on, men and women knew the Energy Ball was their connection to God, and essential for their Spiritual well-being on Planet Earth!

Men and women lived happily with the Energy Ball for a very long time, until one day a fool said, "There is nothing between your hands," and the population believed him. This led to the Energy Ball becoming unpopular and often forbidden!

The lack of connection to Life Energy led humanity away from God and into conflicts, hatred, violence, murder, and wars. This created a Spiritual Fog that obscured God's view of humanity.

God then said, "Why didn't they continue with Energy Ball!?"

Because of the Spiritual Fog, God could only contact and participate with tiny parts of humanity. These amazing experiences brought God a little hope for humanity maturing to a respectful species on Planet Earth, and left God with a deep, deep longing to participate and share more often in the lives of Radiant Human Beings!

Suddenly, in one area the fog was dissipating! God was thrilled!!! Through this opening, God witnessed a magnificent scene! Men and women, of all ages and with different colored skin, gathered in a circle and in the center, holding a Giant Energy Ball!

God was overwhelmed and started to cry. These tears dripped down upon the people in golden colored light! This gave these people evidence that God heard their Blessings, which built a great strength, excitement and confidence in the community.

Humanity was not alone. There was still the possibility to heal Planet Earth and create World Peace!

With vigor, God sent Angels out in the billions to encourage Energy Ball for Peace Ceremonies, and to help dissipate humanity's Spiritual Fog. This guidebook is your invitation.

Section 5
Personal Growth

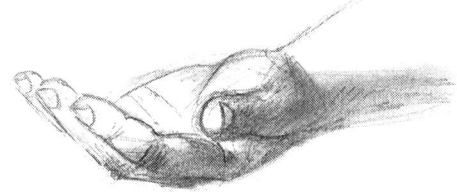

Chapter 14
Daily Routine with the Energy Ball

Adding the Energy Ball to your planned activities assists with a smooth and enjoyable day.

- Waking Up
- Starting your Day
- Lunch Break with the Energy Ball
- Aging Gracefully with the Energy Ball
- Preparation for Sacred Sleep
- Deep Meditative Sleep

Waking Up

When we wake up from sleeping, there is an adjustment time as our spirit and body realign.

Utilizing the Energy Ball is a simple way to guide you into your day.

1. After waking up, form an Energy Ball in the Charging position.

2. Bless and welcome your day by stating your intention. Use these words, or create your own Blessing:

   What a joy it is to be alive today! I am ready to experience what life will bring me throughout all the moments of this day. I am thankful for the air I am breathing. (Take a deep breath!) I open my heart and feel Life's Essence moving through me. Wow!! What a great honor to be a Human Being on Planet Earth today!

3. Gently blow into the Energy Ball, and deepen your intention:

As my spirit arises, I smile as Life's essence surges through my body, enlivening every molecule with Light, bringing forth my passion for Life! I am ready to be guided to meet wonderful, amazing people so that as a team, we can feed the Spiritual Peace. I am ready for whatever will come forth this day. I'm excited!

4. Invite our Sun's magical essence into you and the adventures of your day by looking at the Sunrise, or the first glimpse of Sunlight that you see after you rise up from your bed, through the Energy Ball.

5. Joyfully, spread the Energy Ball around your body, and be ready for new sacred adventures!

6. Rinse your hands and face with water or take a shower.

Starting your Day

In this activity, the Energy Ball creates a womb for your daily agenda, allowing the vibrations of your planned activities to organize.

1. Write down the activities that you plan you do today. Be as detailed as you wish.

2. Form an Energy Ball in the Charging position.

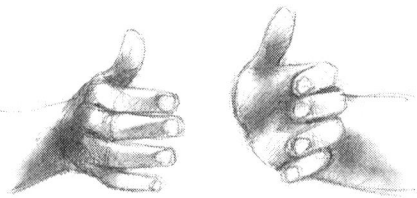

3. Express your intention for the day with a Blessing:

Thank you, Creator, for the opportunity to be alive today and to breathe this sacred breath of life! I am available to bring forth Light through all my activities today on this beautiful Planet Earth! I welcome you and my Angelic Friends to participate with me in today's adventures!

4. Place the Energy Ball around your plan.

5. With a positive, passionate, successful voice, read your entire list out loud, go steadily from event to event.

6. Bring your attention to one activity at a time, and give it your specific Blessing by saying a few keywords about it into the Energy Ball.

7. With your breath, blow Life Energy into the Energy Ball, allowing it to surround this planned activity with your Blessing.

8. When you complete all the events that you wish to Bless, place the Energy Ball around your body. At the same time, imagine yourself doing your planned activities in a positive, joyful and successful manner.

9. Be happy, you're ready for the day, with a daily plan charged with Life Energy!

During the day, form Energy Balls often and remember your intention for the day, noticing how the Energy Ball has affected the outcome of those events.

This is your day to shine your Light. Only you can bring Life's Passion into your day's activities. Others can stimulate you, but it is up to you to have a vibrant successful day.

For any obstacles that may come up, use the Energy Ball to flow through them smoothly.

Lunch Break with the Energy Ball

During the middle of the day make a connection to the Spirit of Life with the Energy Ball.

A few activities to use:

- Waterfall of Liquid Light ~ reference page (21).
- Hand Massage ~ reference page (43).
- Mirror ~ Energy Ball ~ reference page (53).
- Adjusting Overall Energy Body ~ reference page (55).
- Feeding your Joyfulness ~ reference page (62).
- Blessing Food ~ reference page (47).
- Energy Ball Using Your Feet ~ reference page (43).

You may also invite one or more friends, family members, and work associates to form an Energy Ball with you. If they have never made one, go to *Chapter 2, Creating the Energy Ball*[61].

Aging Gracefully with the Energy Ball

Our bodies change and grow older day by day by day......

Bring vitality into the aging process with this activity:

1. Form an Energy Ball in the Nurturing position, place it over your heart, and love yourself.

2. Allow your breathing to be slow and rhythmic.

3. Move the Energy Ball downwards so that it is over and directing Life Energy into your abdomen, Sense how this nurturing Energy spreads throughout this region of your body.

4. Bring the Energy Ball down lower towards your hips. With the Radiant position, direct Life Energy towards your feet. Sense how the whole lower part of your body fills with light.

5. Move your hands upwards so they radiate into your

---

61 *See Chapter 2, page 16.*

shoulders. Sense how Life Energy rises up in your body.

6. Bring your hands so that they are around your head, stimulating your brain and your intelligence!

7. Move your hands above your head radiating downwards towards your entire body. Sense how your Spirit is happy.

8. Say a Blessing of thankfulness to be alive today on Planet Earth, then rinse your hands and face in water.

Complaining about aging confuses you; nurturing yourself brings you into reality.

After you learn how to move the Energy Ball around your body, create your own Ceremony.

Preparation for Sacred Sleep

Before going into the rejuvenating time of sleep, prepare yourself by reviewing your day's events. This allows your thinking process to organize and slow down, making your consciousness available for Life's magical healing process to work while sleeping.

1. Form an Energy Ball in the Nurturing position.

2. Review your day's activities, one event at a time. Allow the focused Energy from the Ball to feed and organize the vibrations of each event.

3. Ask yourself: what was the quality of my Energy and my attitude during that event? Does the Energy Ball want to shrink or expand? What type of experience was it: radiant, strong, passive, happy, joyful, weak, sad, angry, inquiring, boring or interesting? It is okay not to know what to think of an event.

4. One-by-one, go through your day's events and allow them time to complete in your thinking process, thereby blessing

them.

5. Notice which events feel unfinished. Write down what you need to do to complete them, while saying that you will address them the next day or whenever the appropriate time arises.

6. Gaze into the Energy Ball, and say a word of thankfulness for the opportunity to experience Life!

7. Move your hands into the Cleansing position, and become deeply thankful for all that you learned and experienced today.

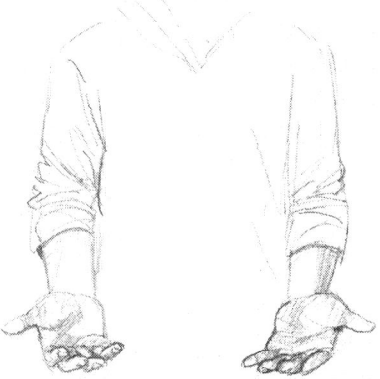

8. Welcome your Angelic Friends to join you on your sleep journey!

9. Appreciate the fact that you have genuinely cared for yourself! You are now ready to have a Sacred Sleep............

Deep Meditative Sleep

When the body enters into a deep meditative sleep, the brain's wavelengths slow down. This allows the body systems to naturally care for themselves, and provides space for development and transformation. This restorative and healing sleep in also Creator's classroom, where you may learn about yourself and your journey on Planet Earth.

1. Perform the previous activity, *Preparation for a Sacred Sleep*, beforehand.

2. Lie down on your back, comfortably in bed, make sure your head is well supported and even with your body.

3. Form an Energy Ball in the Nurturing position, and let it intensify.

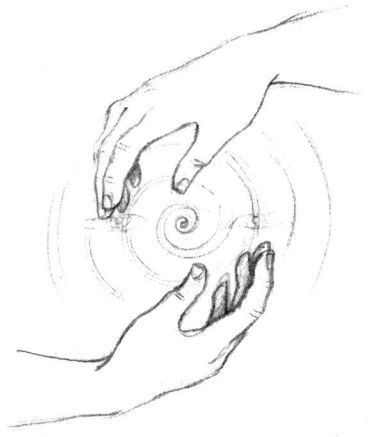

4. Focus yourself by dimming your Perception Switch[62].

5. Hold the Energy Ball over your solar plexus, and allow the nerves of your body to relax and release the tension from your day's activities while saying a few calming words to yourself.

---

62   *See Energy Ball as a Perception Switch, page 165*

6. Guide Life Energy through your nervous system by blowing into the Energy Ball. Intend that the Energy Ball enters into and flows through the nerves of your solar plexus and into your organs, glands, muscles and tissues.

7. Notice how this makes your cells happy and you feel like smiling. It is a good time to acknowledge that, right now, you love and appreciate yourself!

8. Move your hands so they face upwards and by your side.

9. Use these words to guide yourself into a deep meditative sleep:

   Imagine yourself calmly walking along a beach or beautiful nature trail. Look at the beautiful scenery, listen to the sounds of the birds, water and wind. Smell the air and notice that you feel relaxed and tuned into Nature.

   You're attracted to a beautiful location, and lie down and relax. An Angel comes over to you and asks you what you would like to learn while you are sleeping. You are taken over to a giant Library of Experiences and invited to explore and learn....

10. Say a Blessing to and thank Creator for your opportunity to learn more about being a Human Angel on Planet Earth while you are sleeping.

11. Keep yourself in the place of awake and asleep for as long as possible. This accentuates the restorative and healing power of your resting time, and prepares you for learning.

Chapter 15: Personal Training

Use the Energy Ball as a guide to deepen and enrich the quality of your Life experiences.

- Becoming Skillful with the Energy Ball
- In the Flow of Life Position
- Ray of Life Energy Position
- Toning and the Energy Ball
- Spiritual Sight Development

Becoming Skillful with the Energy Ball

With consistency, we develop our skill with the Energy Ball, and learn to use to it wisely and gain assurance.

Thoughts on how to become skillful:

- Notice when your hands instinctively form an Energy Ball and seek to understand why.
- Allow the Energy Ball to become an important part of your life's daily activities and develop into a natural, healthy habit.
- Actively pay attention to what the Energy Ball says each time you form one.
- Often during the day, expand the Energy Ball around your body, Blessing yourself.
- Notice how your body registers the event of forming an Energy Ball as a healing experience.
- Become confident with connecting to Creator and your Angelic Friends by practicing encoding the Energy Ball with Blessing.

In the Flow of Life Position

When we are in the Flow of Life, we say the right thing in the right moment, and easily handle whatever comes up with confidence.

This position channels abundant Life Energy to flow through the physical body.

1. Form an Energy Ball in the Charging position, and allow it to build up in intensity.

2. Place one of your hands with the palm facing upwards at waist height. This is the receiving hand. Sense Energy entering your hand from Creator.

3. Then, place the other hand with the palm facing outwards at shoulder height. This is the sending hand. Sense Life Energy flowing as it moves outwards from the body.

4. Notice that you receive and give Life Energy, and all your body fills up with Light!

5. Say a Blessing of thankfulness to Creator for your ability to flow with Life's consistent gift of Energy.

6. Move your hands into the Light Connection position, and experience being in a channel of Light.

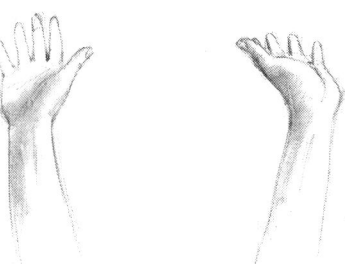

7. Pay attention to how everything around you is brighter from the intensity of the Energy you transmit.

8. Notice how the Universal Flow of Life moves throughout and around your body, Blessing you!

9. Move your hands into the Cleansing position, and make the affirmation, "I wish to be in the flow of life consistently!!"

Ray of Light Energy Position

Use this position to intensely focus Life Energy[63]:

1. Form an Energy Ball in the Nurturing position. Let it build up in intensity for a minute.

2. Gently bend your wrist and raise the top hand so that the two hands form an "L" shape. The top palm faces forward, and the bottom palm faces upwards.

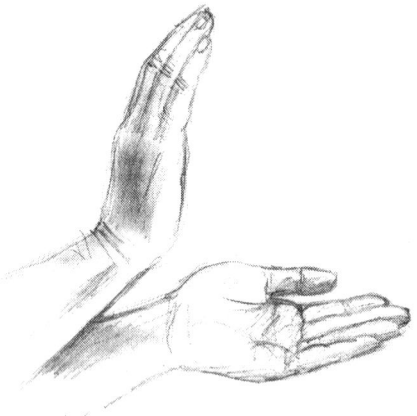

3. Sense the Energy from both hands merging together and sending out a Beam of Light in the direction that your hands are facing.

4. Focus your attention on one specific place. With your intention, send your Ray of Light towards it.

5. By maintaining this position, you develop the ability to send out increased Life Energy from your hands.

6. Slowly move your hands to another location.

7. Notice that as you move your hands the Ray of Light leaves

---

63 *See Ray of Light, page 126.*

a trail of Light that nourishes and Blesses each place where your hands are focused[64].

8. Move your hands into the Cleansing position, and know that this focused Light is your gift, and a great Blessing to our world!

Toning and the Energy Ball

When we make a sound, air moves through the vocal folds, (vocal cords) and creates a vibration, a wave, that it is heard as a sound. Toning is sending out a continuous wave of Energy. Each specific tone carries its own unique vibrational code.

When we combine Toning with the Energy Ball we have the ability to create specific vibrations for specific purposes.

This enhanced vibration can be used for cleansing, nourishing ourselves and others, clearing impure vibrations, and sending Blessings.

My friend Jeanne White Eagle gives this advice before she guides a group singing, "Create a song, no words, no thought, only the intent of love. Don't think, just make the sound". And her husband John Pehrson says, "I have come to think of sound as an effective carrier of intention." These words also apply to Toning.

There are numerous ways and techniques to tone, here is a simple practice with the Energy Ball:

1. Form an Energy Ball in the Charging position.

2. Blow into the Energy Ball and allow it to go around your body, creating a Safe Space for you to tone.

3. Prepare yourself by taking a deep breath and exhaling saying *aaahhhh.*

64　See Ceremony to Bless Humanity, page 184.

4. Notice the tone vibrating inside the Energy Ball, and how it affects your vocal cords. Repeat this *aaahhhh* tone several times.

5. Try Toning each of the vowel sound (a, e, i o, u), and repeat them over and over, directing their vibration into the Energy Ball.

6. After you become acquainted with these tones, go to a very low pitch and notice how this vibration has a heavier effect on the Energy Ball.

7. To have a lighter effect on the Energy Ball, go to a very high pitch. It makes my Energy Ball tingle!

8. Then go between very low and very high pitches. Sense how this stimulates and enlivens your vocal folds.

9. Play around with your voice and see which tones are pleasant, neutral, and repel you.

10. Choose a tone that has a pleasant vibration and attracts you. Repeat it over and over for a few minutes.

11. Direct this tone into the Energy Ball. Enjoy how it opens your heart and sparkles with pleasant vibrations, filling you up with satisfaction!

12. Continue to tone, as you place the Energy Ball around you by bringing it above your head and slowly moving it downwards to surround your shoulders, chest, and abdomen until your feet, enveloping your entire body.

13. Enjoy! You are now surrounded and Blessed by your pleasant Tone vibration!

14. Rinse your hands in water to give them a fresh start!

The vibrations felt inside the Ball have meaning to me:

- Neutral tones help me with internal organization, bring me satisfaction, and are helpful for me to contain my Energy.

- Pleasant and attractive tones enhance my radiant output of Life Energy, make me smile, laugh, and are fulfilling.

- Repelling tones dissolve old, stuck vibrations from my body. They are sometimes uncomfortable and unpleasant, but promote healing!

The next step is Toning with a group. To do this, see the topic, *Collective Chanting*[65].

Spiritual Sight Development

Developing Spiritual Sight is a personal adventure. I have found that the Energy Ball has made it an easier and a more precise journey[66].

- **Exercise A** ~ Seeing into the Energy Ball
- **Exercise B** ~ Seeing the Essence of Life
- **Exercise C** ~ Energy Ball as a Perception Switch
- **Exercise D** ~ Monitoring with the Energy Ball

Exercise A ~ Seeing into the Energy Ball

1. Form an Energy Ball in the Charging position, looking very deeply into it. Take your time.

2. With unfocused vision, stare into the Ball, concentrating on seeing what is in the space between your hands.

3. Use your peripheral vision to widen your perception. This makes it easier to see the Energy clusters moving around inside the Ball. They look like puffy dots and waves of light.

---

65   *See Collective Chanting, page 95.*
66   *See Spiritual Sight, page 132.*

This practice turns on the eye's ability to peer into the invisible world.

Exercise B ~ Seeing the Essence of Life

1. Look into the sky where the Sun is not shining brightly.
2. Focus your eyes and attention so that you look in-between the sky and yourself.
3. Notice the little dots moving around. They look like very bright tiny Suns that are everywhere and moving very quickly!
4. By trying to focus on one dot at a time, you stimulate your ability to use your Spiritual Sight.
5. Now that you know what they look like, in the correct lighting they can be noticed everywhere!
6. Known by many names, I call these little dots the *Essence of Life*, and believe they are life substance that is available for utilization, and part of Sunlight.

Viewing the Essence of Life opens up our ability to see into the Spiritual Atmosphere of the Invisible World. This is where

Angels, Spiritual Energy, and Universal Knowledge abide.

While I was editing this exercise, I was looking at the Essence of Life in the sky to make sure I was explaining the exercise correctly, and heard the call of an Eagle. Then for several minutes I watched the Essence of Life as the background for the flying Eagle. I could see that the Eagle's Overall Energy Body was much larger than its physical body.

Exercise C ~ Energy Ball as a Perception Switch

The Energy Ball has the ability to adjust your Spiritual Sight by turning it into a Perception Switch. Visualize a round light dimmer switch that adjusts the amount of electricity received in a light fixture. Apply this image to how you control your Spiritual Sight. This switch has the ability to intensify, dim, expand, and contract the amount you perceive.

Use this activity to practice turning your Spiritual Sight into a Perception Switch:

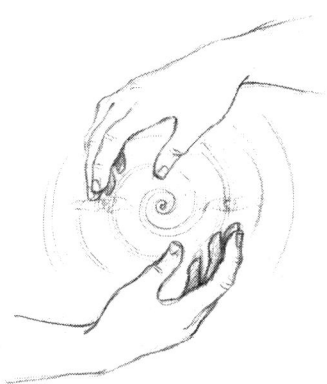

1. Form an Energy Ball in the Charging position.
2. Visualize the Perception Switch.
3. Turn the Energy Ball to the right, and notice how your perception and awareness increases. Your Overall Energy

Body enlarges, and you become very sensitive and aware of everything around you.

4. Turn the Energy Ball to the left, and notice how your perception is pulled inwards. You feel more introspective and contained, the size of your Overall Energy Body has reduced, and you are much less sensitive to outside vibrations.

5. Bring the Perception Switch to the Ready position, which is in the middle. Notice that you perceive both the invisible and physical worlds simultaneously, and that you are available for new incoming information.

6. Experiment with using the Energy Ball as your Perception Switch, and notice what it feels like to have your Spiritual Sight under your control.

7. Move your hands into the Cleansing position for a minute.

8. Say a Blessing in appreciation for your Spiritual Sight and your ability to control it. Then rinse your hands in water.

This training builds confidence, enabling you to handle situations gracefully.

I turn my Spiritual Perception switch to:

- Wide open, when I am in an energetically pure environment and feel adventurous.

- Semi-open, when I am occupied with a task, sense impure vibrations, and am in a crowded place.

- Most of the time, I keep my Perception Switch in the Ready position, so I am available for fresh incoming information.

Exercise D ~ Monitoring with the Energy Ball

In this exercise, the Energy Ball is utilized to perceive what is

spiritually *in or out of tune.* Sensing
Energy opens a channel to what is
happening with the Life Energy in
and around ourselves, and stimulates
our ability to use our Spiritual Sight.

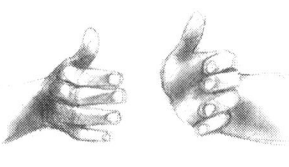

1. Form an Energy Ball in the Charging position.

2. Pay attention to the sensation between your hands and
   acknowledge what you are perceiving.

3. After a minute, move your hands into the Ray of Light
   position[67].

4. Look at and project a beam of
   Energy at whatever you wish
   to sense: an object, situation, or
   person.

5. Instantly, a vibrational wave of
   Energy returns back to your hands
   and eyes. This flow of Energy is
   encoded with information, and can be understood with your
   intuition.

6. A few questions to ask yourself: What does the Energy feel
   like? Is it *in or out of tune?* Pure or impure? What comes to
   mind? What does your intuition tell you to do? What does
   it feel like?

7. Rinsing your hands in water often during this practice helps
   you to be more perceptive.

These exercises assist in opening the eyes' physical ability to
see Life Energy. They provide the opportunity to dissipate
the interference around Spiritual Sight. As our Spiritual Sight
develops, it becomes a powerful Life tool that assists us to live
a sacred life.

---

67   *See Ray of Light Position, page 160.*

Chapter 16: Assistance

To make your life experience smoother and more transformative, include the Energy Ball! Life's journey has countless opportunities where assistance is needed.

- Gifting the Energy Ball
- Nurturing Thoughts with a Wish
- Traveling with the Energy Ball
- Relieving Pain with the Energy Ball
- Calming the Emotions
- Repairing Collapsed Energy Fields

Gifting the Energy Ball

To nurture and Bless someone you care about, surround them in Healing Life Energy with the Energy Ball. This is a strong experience. Therefore, ask them or their guardian beforehand for their willingness to participate. This gift can be given from any distance.

1. Form an Energy Ball in the Charging position, and focus your sight into the space between your hands.

2. With your Spiritual Sight, notice Life Energy flowing inside the Energy Ball.

3. Envision the recipient inside your Energy Ball. It is helpful to look at their picture, read some of their words, recall experiences you have shared. The object is to connect to their Spiritual Essence.

4. With a Blessing, welcome in Creator and your Angelic Friends to surround the recipient, and then say some words to honor them, words that assist their body, mind and emotions to work together as a team.

5. With your intention, invite Life's healing effect to spread quickly through the cells of the recipient's body.

6. Blow a long slow breath into the Energy Ball. At the same time, gracefully move your hands into the Radiant position.

7. Envision the Energy Ball traveling to the recipient, surrounding and caring for them. Notice that they are in a Safe Space!

8. Hold this position until you sense they are sufficiently Blessed. It usually is between 5- 30 minutes.

9. Rinse your hands in water afterwards.

10. Contact the recipient and inquire as to how deeply they were able to receive the gift.

Nurturing Thoughts with a Wish

Wishing combined with the Energy Ball, creates a fertile atmosphere for your thoughts to become reality. Wishing is the beginning of creation. It sends out a wave of Energy that has the possibility to ripple into reality.

1. Form an Energy Ball in the Nurturing position.

2. Focus your attention on your hands, noticing everything: your fingers, nails, lines, color, texture, and the Energy surrounding them. Genuinely appreciate your hands. Move them around noticing their versatility!

3. Say a few words aloud to describe something you wish to nurture, such as: "I wish for World Peace." (This activity is not for wishing for material gains.)

4. Invite the vibration of the wish to enter and circulate around the Energy Ball.

5. Notice there is increased activity between your hands with a charged vibration.

6. Bring thankfulness into the wish, such as *"I am very thankful to be alive today and to have the wisdom and desire for human beings to live Peacefully together."*

7. Welcome Creator and your Angelic Friends to join you by saying a Blessing.

8. Gently blow your thankfulness into the Energy Ball.

9. Notice how the thankful vibration begins to nourish your thoughts. They can be sensed in the hands as tiny Energy Balls bouncing around.

10. Again, state your intention out loud with a strong affirmation, directing it into the Energy Ball: *"Yes, I am going to stimulate World Peace!"* This affirms the Energetic atmosphere, and charges it with your power!

11. When you sense the wish is clear, place it into your consciousness by holding the Energy Ball around your head with the intention of your wish becoming reality.

12. Then bring the Energy Ball downwards towards your feet, and surround your body with the vibration of your wish.

13. After a minute, extend your hands upwards into the Light Connection position as far as they can reach, and allow your energized wish to expand and expand and expand!

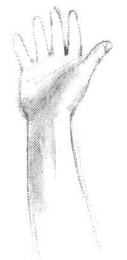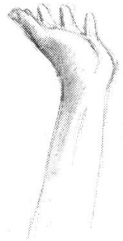

Traveling with the Energy Ball

Include the Energy Ball in your packing list! It will make your journey smoother and more enjoyable.

1. Write down the major steps of your upcoming journey, from leaving your home, arriving at your destination, and then returning home. Include: walking, driving, flying, where you will rest and sleep, the places you wish to visit and the people you plan to meet, and with whom you would like to form an Energy Ball. Add as many details as you wish.

2. Form an Energy Ball in the Nurturing position.

3. Place your list in front of you so that it is easily readable.

4. Visualize yourself being shrunk in size and inside the Energy Ball.

5. Say out loud the first item on your list and imagine yourself going through this activity.

6. Notice how this affects the Energy between your hands.

7. Go step-by-step through your journey and notice the increased flow through the Energy Ball, organizing each step and creating **Preparation Energy** for travels.

8. Pay attention to the different nuances of Energy and the emotions that arise inside you as you go step-by-step through your journey.

9. Bless yourself by placing the Energy Ball around your body, noticing your excitement about your upcoming travel opportunity. Have wonderful adventures!

A little more:

- Envision yourself with plenty of Life Energy, a smile on your face, feeling ready and available to do whatever is you need to do.

- Decide in advance where and when it can be helpful to form an Energy Ball and which activity to use. Remember that you may also spontaneously form an Energy Ball.

- Prepare yourself for new adventures, and tell yourself that you do not have to repeat unpleasant past travel experiences.

- If you anticipate challenges, move your hands into the Cleansing position, and envision yourself having a victory and easily flowing through these experiences.

Relieving Pain with the Energy Ball

These activities clarify the body's internal communication channels by guiding soothing and healing Life Energy into the painful area of your body with the Energy Ball. They form an energetic connection between the nerves and the hormones. By repeating these exercises, your body learns to control pain.

There are always reasons for pain. If the reasons for pain are not addressed, these pain relief activities will be limited in the length of time they last.

Rinsing your hands in water often during these activities quickens the healing process. Each part follows the previous one before it:

- **Part A** ~ Relaxing the Body
- **Part B** ~ Accessing Internal Healing Power
- **Part C** ~ Surrounding the Pain
- **Part D** ~ Internal Communication

Part A ~ Relaxing the Body

1. Form an Energy Ball in the Nurturing position, and hold it over your solar plexus.

2. Bring your attention and the Energy from the Ball to this complex of nerve and its connections throughout your abdomen.

3. Gently and steadily blow into the Energy Ball, increasing its intensity of Life Energy.

4. Say a Blessing of thankfulness to Creator for your physical body's ability to heal itself. Welcome in your Angelic Friends to assist you in this healing process.

5. Visualize the Energy from the Ball traveling throughout your body, relaxing the nerves around your solar plexus clarifying your internal connections.

Part B ~ Accessing Internal Healing Power

When the quantity of protective hormones running through the body is lowered, the body's natural healing process is stimulated, and pain recedes.

1. Form an Energy Ball in the Charging position, holding the Energy Ball over your solar plexus.

2. Explain to yourself that pain does not mean an emergency, and request your pituitary gland to inform the adrenal glands to slow down the production of protective hormones. Trust your *master gland*; it knows how to send the message!

3. Move one hand over your forehead, and connect to your pituitary gland. The other hand is over the solar plexus and connects to your adrenal glands.

4. Hold your hands in this position for a few minutes with the intention of these two glands communicating and sending out pain controlling hormones.

Part C ~ Surrounding the Pain

Once you have calmed down and your protective hormones have subsided, you are ready to surround the pain and intensify the amount of healing Life Energy that flows through that part of the body.

1. Form an Energy Ball in the Charging position.

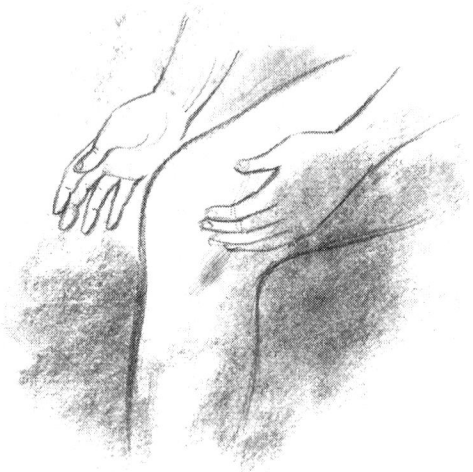

2. Bring your attention to the pain, and move one hand over this area of your body.

3. Place your other hand on the opposite side of your body. For instance, if you are experiencing knee pain, place your hands around your knee so that it is in the middle of the Energy Ball.

4. Notice and allow the muscles and tissues surrounding the painful area to relax and release their tension.

5. Pay attention to what happens inside your entire body.

6. Blow a steady stream of air into the Energy Ball and your knee, intensifying the healing activity.

Your body will tell you how close it wants your hands to be from the pain. As the pain lessens, bring your hands closer to your body, almost touching, and notice how your body loves to absorb this Healing Energy.

If at any time the pain increases, move your hands further away until you find a comfortable distance for you.

Part D ~ Internal Communication

Increase the speed of your recovery by assisting your body's internal feedback communication channels to clarify.

1. Form an Energy Ball in the Nurturing position holding it over your solar plexus, with the intention of connecting to your inner healing power through your adrenal glands.

2. When you sense an initial calming of your body, move one hand over the painful area. This opens up a communication channel between the adrenal glands and the painful area.

3. After a minute or two, move your hand back over the solar plexus, giving it fresh Energetic information from the pain.

4. Again, move your hand back over the painful area and intensify the Healing Life Energy with slow rhythmic breathing.

5. Move back and forth several times, noticing that the body's internal healing process soothes your pain.

6. To conclude, bring the Energy Ball over your head and spread it around your body, helping integrate the changes.

Trust your self-healing ability, and become accustomed to overcoming your pain.

After these activities, take a shower to relax your muscles and calm your nerves. This will help accelerate the healing process. If you feel tired, care for yourself by taking a nap.

If the pain does not lessen, remember to seek medical advice. These Pain Relief activities are not a substitute for medical advice or treatment. Consult with your physician and ask if the Energy Ball will benefit you.

Calming the Emotions

When the emotions are under the control of Life they are amazing! Pleasurable hormones such as endorphins, serotonin, dopamine, and oxytocin rush through the body making us feel wonderful! When the emotions are out of control, unclear

messages are given that mix up the natural hormonal secretions creating confusion and lots of problems.

In this activity, the Energy Ball stabilizes and calms down Emotional Energy by surrounding and Blessing the heart with Life Energy.

1. Find a place where you can be alone and comfortable, preferably in Nature.

2. Form an Energy Ball in the Nurturing position, and allow it to build up in intensity.

3. Bring your attention to the way in which you are breathing.

4. Move the Energy Ball, and sway your body gently from side to side.

5. Take a deep breath and strongly exhale making the sound *aaahhhh*. Repeat this sound a few times.

6. Stimulate a healing vibration by thinking about someone you love to spend time with, or something that you enjoy doing that brings you pleasure. Say a few keywords about them or the activity, and direct this vibration into the Energy Ball. This encodes the Energy Ball with a Healing Vibration.

7. Place the Energy Ball an arm's length in front of you with your hands facing your chest. Notice the encoded Life Energy filling up the space between your hands, arms, and chest.

8. Exhale strongly, releasing tension from your body by inviting and guiding the Energy from the Ball to enter into the cells of your chest, lungs, heart, thymus, ribs, muscles, tissues, and nerves.

9. Pay attention to how your breathing has changed, and how your heart is surrounded in Light Energy!

10. After about a minute, very slowly move your hands and the Energy Ball so they are above your heart.

11. Visualize Life Energy flowing deeply into your heart and the fluid of the protective sac around the heart, the pericardium. Fill these areas with calming, healing Life Energy!

12. Inhale several times with the specific intention that Life Energy will enter deep into your entire body and stabilize your emotions.

13. Pay attention to your renewed Heart Energy spreading inside of your entire body.

14. Form another Energy Ball in the Charging position, build up its intensity, and then Bless yourself by placing the Energy Ball around your body.

15. Move your hands into the Cleansing position. Notice how you are more connected to yourself and in a calmer space.

16. To deepen the activity, form Energy Balls often for the next few hours, days, years....

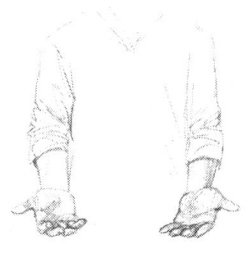

Personal Story

It was the 1970's. I was in college and still learning how to maintain my Personal Radiance in an energetically polluted society.

One day, I was very confused and had an internal emotional problem, so I decided to call an amazing man I had just met, Lou Rotola, and ask him for guidance. As soon as he heard my voice, he said with vigor, "Jeff, great you called!! Would you like to join me when I give a presentation on Ontology today at Queens College?" I said "Yes," and hung up the phone. I could not remember why I called him! His *Excitement for Life* instantly pulled me out of my emotional problem. Ever since, whenever I get low, I remember this story, and nowadays, I also form an Energy Ball.

Repairing Collapsed Energy Fields

This activity uses the breath and Energy Ball to *pop out* a compressed, collapsed, or deflated Overall Energy Body. It creates a Safe Space around the body, and provides increased Life Energy to fill and recharge the physical body.

The evidence that the Overall Energy Body has deflated is that you feel closed in, small, limited, squashed, exhausted and without Energy.

1. Form an Energy Ball in the Charging position.

2. With a steady breath, slowly and delicately blow into the Energy Ball, building the density of Energy within the Ball.

3. Notice how it spreads into your

entire body.

4. Keep blowing into the Energy Ball. If your hands want to move further apart, resist the urge for the time being, so the Energy has time to intensify.

5. When you sense the Energy Ball is ready to burst, take a deep breath and quickly blow into the Energy Ball with force.

6. Your hands will automatically spread out wide as the Energy Ball expands around your Body.

7. Your Overall Energy Body has just *popped out!*

8. Keep your hands stationary for a minute, and allow your Overall Energy Body to fill up with Light Energy.

9. Repeat this activity a few times and then do the *Adjusting the Overall Energy Body* activity[68].

---

68   *See Adjusting the Overall Energy Body, page 55.*

Chapter 17
Individual Energy Ball Ceremonies

- About Ceremony
- Ceremony to Hug Planet Earth
- Ceremony to Bless Humanity
- Ceremony to Cleanse Impure Earth Energy
- Pet's Energy Ball Ceremony
- Walking Ceremony
- Strengthening Ceremony
- Energy Ball Dance Ceremony

About Ceremony

Ceremony is a sacred opportunity to focus our attention and connect to the power of the Spirit.

How a person enters into and transitions out of a Ceremony is vital to creating a genuine experience.

Some reminders:

- Rinse your hands with water before, after, and sometimes during the Ceremony Time.
- Invite Creator and your Angelic Friends to participate with you by saying a Blessing.
- Bring yourself into the present moment by paying attention to your breath. (Actually, in every moment we participate in a Breathing Ceremony!)
- Notice that you are connected to Planet Earth through your feet.
- Guide your thoughts to recede into the background of your awareness, allowing your full consciousness to be available for the Ceremony.

- Shift into a perceptive mode, noticing and honoring your emotions.

- Conclude your Ceremony by taking a few steps forwards, symbolizing the transition out of Ceremony time.

- Thank yourself for your willingness to participate in the Ceremony.

Ceremony to Hug Planet Earth

Planet Earth has become damaged from humanity's over exploitation, and really, really needs our Love and Blessing! This Hug supports and feeds Planet Earth with Loving, Hopeful Energy!

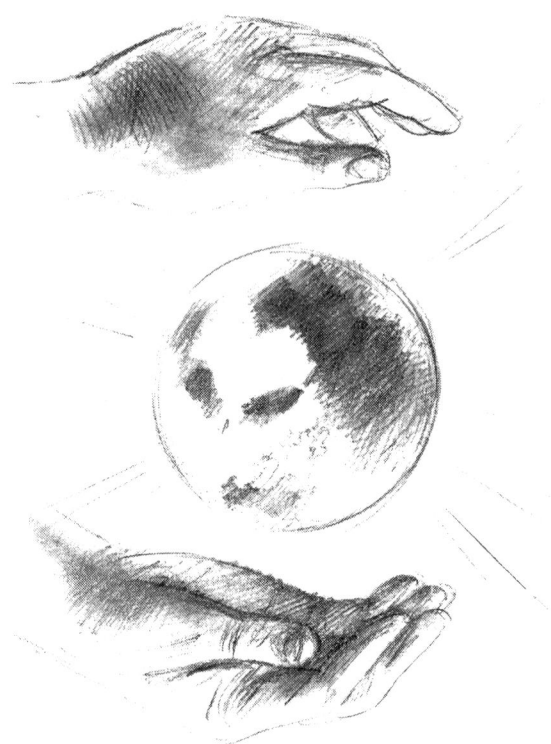

1. Make a solid connection to Planet Earth by using the Grounding position.

2. Notice the sensation in your body, and how it becomes heavier and fills up with the Earth's vibration.

3. Move your hands into the Charging position, and allow sufficient time to develop a strong flow of Life Energy in your hands.

4. Visualize a very Small Planet Earth that fits in between your hands, and inside the Energy Ball.

5. Nourish yourself and Planet Earth by imagining Light Energy coming in from the top of your head, through your pineal gland, channeled through your whole body, and intensifying the flow of Life Energy coming out of your hands, feeding Small Planet Earth.

6. Sense how the Energy Ball gets bigger and more vibrant!

7. Say a Blessing of appreciation to Planet Earth:

   Thank you, Creator for this beautiful, wonderful, amazing, abundant, Sacred Planet upon which I am privileged to live. During this Ceremony, I offer my Light Energy and deepest love for all the abundance that Planet Earth offers!

8. Intensify the Energy Ball with one strong powerful breath directed into the Miniature Planet Earth between your hands.

9. Visualize the Energy flowing into Planet Earth's crevices, and seeping deep down into its core. Pay attention to how you are feeding Planet Earth with Life Energy!

10. Move your arms and hands outwards. This creates a larger Energy Ball between your chest, hands and arms, allowing the Small Planet Earth to grow and fill the space.

11. Give a slight squeeze, hugging Planet Earth, saying and giving your unique Blessing of Love and Appreciation.

12. Notice that you instantly receive a very strong burst of Light Energy from Planet Earth and your Heart smiles!

13. Send a calming vibration to Planet Earth by blowing a gentle stream of air into the Energy Ball; and remember the image of soft, green, lush moss as Light Energy flows deep into the ground.

14. Sense how Planet Earth is blessed and a little bit happier and Peaceful!

15. Using the Grounding position, place the Energy Ball into the Planet Earth in a ceremonious way.

16. Guide this sacred Energy with a Blessing, and notice how it spreads and revitalizes Planet Earth.

17. Move your hands into the Cleansing position, and acknowledge and appreciate the fact that you just nurtured Planet Earth!

Ceremony to Bless Humanity

Humanity has gone off track from Creator's Purity. This is very, very sad, but it is our collective reality.

This ceremony helps to steer Humanity back on course:

1. Create an intention for the Ceremony using these elements. Be as specific as you wish:

   • Assist human beings to wake up from their Spiritual sleep, and develop a solid connect to their own inner purity.

- Create harmony and friendship between human beings, no matter where and to whom they are born.

- Plant Peaceful Light seeds that spread into every community on Planet Earth.

- Invite humanity to pop out of its current spiritually restricted condition, into its rightful place as Planet Earth's overseer and caretaker.

2. Choose a natural elevated location where you have a panoramic view, or as near as you can find. An ideal spot is on the peak of a hill or mountain with a 360-degree view. During this Ceremony, you will move in a clockwise circle, and stop and Bless the four directions.

3. Form an Energy Ball in the Charging position.

4. Take time and let it intensify by focusing and grounding yourself with your intention.

5. Say a Blessing of Thankfulness to Creator for this opportunity to share Light Energy.

6. Shift to the Radiant position, becoming conscious of your hands sending out Life Energy.

7. Intensify the current of Life Energy coming out of your hands by imagining Light Energy coming in from the top of your head, entering into your pineal gland and flowing through your entire body, coming out of your hands, and being sent in the direction that you are facing.

8. Focus on guiding Life Energy towards everything in the direction that you are facing: Nature, buildings, cities, countries, water bodies, animals, people, enveloping all in your radiant Light!

9. Concentrate on the people living there, think about those you know who live in that direction, and send them your Light Blessings!

10. Keep in mind your intention as you say out loud everything that you wish to Bless. Take your time and be thorough.

11. When you sense that you have sufficiently Blessed this direction, move clockwise to the next direction, and continue to send your Radiate Light.

12. After you have finished all four directions, recall some of the feelings and vibrations from your experience in each direction, and encode them into the Energy Ball.

13. Say a Blessing and ceremoniously place the Energy Ball into Planet Earth by using the Grounding position.

14. Move your hands into the Cleansing position for as long as you wish. Then rinse your hands in water.

I often do this Ceremony on the Mitzpeh Kerem Outlook (Hirbet Hamame) in the Jerusalem Forest, which provides a near 360-degree view of Jerusalem and its surrounding hills.

A few of the places I Bless:

- Facing East: The Old City of Jerusalem, Jericho, the Dead Sea, Jordan, Saudi Arabia, the Indian Ocean.

- Facing South: Bethlehem, Hebron, Eilat, Egypt, the Red Sea, Africa, Antarctic Ocean, the South Pole.

- Facing West: Ein Kerem, Sataf, Tel-Aviv-Yafo, the Mediterranean Sea, Northern Africa, the Atlantic Ocean, the Americas.

- Facing North: Nebi Samuel, Ramallah, Galilee, Lebanon, Europe, the Arctic Ocean, the North Pole.

Ceremony to Cleanse Impure Earth Energy

There are times when I perceive something traumatic has happened in the specific spot where I am standing. It could be fear, confusion, disarray, disharmony, or a disgusting, ugly vibration. This is a signal to me that Planet Earth is wounded and needs attention.

This activity assists Planet Earth by clearing distorted vibrations from inside the ground, and revitalizes the location.

1. Immediately when you sense an Impure Earth Energy, form an Energy Ball in the Charging position.

2. Connect with the core of Planet Earth through your feet, sending your love and appreciation.

3. Welcome Creator and Angels with a Blessing, and feel yourself in a clear space.

4. Intensify the Energy Ball with one strong powerful breath directed into the area between your hands.

5. Connect to pure Earth Energy by moving your hands into the Radiant position, and directing your hands to a pure part of Nature that is near you.

6. After you have made a strong connection, move one of your hands so that it is directed towards the Impure Earth Energy. This creates a pathway for Pure Earth Energy to be sent in and neutralize the impure vibrations.

7. When you sense the connection of Earth Energy between the pure place and the wounded area is flowing, bring both of your hands into the Cleansing position.

8. Say a Blessing, and invite your Angelic Friends to continue to care for this wounded area.

9. Before leaving, notice how the vibration of the area has changed, and that it is returning to send out a purer and purer vibration of Earth Energy.

10. Rinse your hands in water or use the *Waterfall of Liquid Light* [69]activity.

Thank you for assisting Planet Earth and being a conscientious Human Being!!

Pet's Energy Ball Ceremony

Animals instinctively sense the invisible world, and the current of Life Energy. Each animal responds uniquely to the Energy Ball. This ceremony is for dogs and cats. For other pets, adapt the ceremony accordingly.

1. Form an Energy Ball in the Nurturing position.
2. Say a Blessing of Thankfulness for your pet.
3. Gently bring the Energy Ball close to your pet.
4. Pay attention to their reaction: are they curious?
5. Without touching, hold the Energy Ball around your pet, allowing the pet to come smell or nudge against your hands.
6. Notice how your pet reacts and interacts with you.
7. Allow sufficient time for your pet to relax in your Radiant Energy.
8. Move the Energy Ball closer to your pet, and then further

---

69   *See Waterfall of Liquid Light, page 21.*

away a few times, pumping your pet's Overall Energy Body.

9. Change your hands into the Radiant position, and step back several paces. This clears and strengthens your pet's Overall Energy Body.

10. Pay attention to how your pet radiates its Energy Blessing.

11. Bring your hands very close to your pet, almost touching, and feel how both your Overall Energy Bodies blend.

12. As your pet walks around, follow it with your hands, intending that the Light surrounds and Blesses your pet on its journey.

13. Invite your pet to crawl up on your lap or near you, and hold the Energy Ball around it for as long as both of you wish.

After pets are around the Energy Ball for a while, they participate with you and become an Energy Ball Assistant! In group settings, they will often find a place next or in the center of the circle or next to a person who needs assistance.

If your animal is ill, surround and Bless it with the Energy Ball often. This creates a safe space for your pet to heal faster.

If your animal has been mistreated: From a distance, use the Radiant Position to hold a safe, loving space around your pet. Doing this on a consistent basis assists to discharge the effects of the mistreatment.

Walking Ceremony

Walking is vital to living healthily, and assists us in staying connected to Planet Earth. The quality of our experience while walking is enhanced when we utilize the Energy coming out of our feet and hands. These ceremonies guide you into Walking in Harmony with Nature and your True Self.

- **Part A** ~ Preparation
- **Part B** ~ Radiant Walking
- **Part C** ~ Creating a Trail of Light

Part A ~ Preparation

1. Form an Energy Ball in the Charging position, and allow it to build up in intensity.

2. Expand the Energy Ball around your body with a strong breath, and sense how it envelopes your Overall Energy Body.

3. Connect to the Earth Energy by finding a place to sit and form an Energy Ball using your feet[70].

4. Notice how Earth Energy feels solid compared to the fluidness of Life Energy that is felt between your hands.

5. Stand up, shake out your legs, and place your feet completely

---

70   *See Forming an Energy Ball Using your Feet, page 43.*

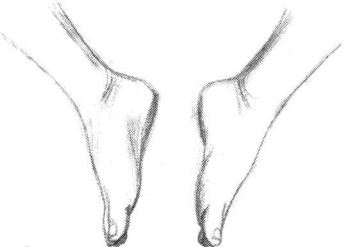

on the ground.

6. With **your** hands in the Radiant position, direct Life Energy into your legs.

7. Say thank you and appreciate your legs for their ability to take you on this journey!

Experience the deep gratitude you have for your body by considering the action of walking. How many parts of your body work together in harmony for you to take one step! Our physical body is amazing! Remember to thank Creator on your journey!

Part B ~ Radiant Walking

1. Start to walk slowly, noticing how you naturally send Life Energy from your feet into the ground. It is very sensational, as if you are bouncing!

2. Intensify the Life Energy flowing through your body and into Planet Earth by imagining Life Energy entering from the top of your head into your pineal gland, and flowing through your entire body.

3. With each step you take, sense Planet Earth responding with a surge of Earth Energy rushing through your feet and your entire body.

4. When you are in the flow of walking, notice that Life Energy continuously cycles into the ground, and then again back up through your body, and back into the ground. This

gives you the bounce in your step.

5. Open your heart in thankfulness for this opportunity that you have to be consciously giving and receiving Earth Energy as you walk!

Part C ~ Creating a Trail of Light

Now that you are walking radiantly, we add your hands.

1. Form an Energy Ball in the Grounding position.

2. Focus your attention on radiating Light Energy from your hands into Planet Earth.

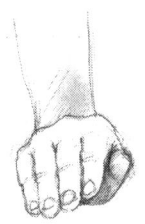 

3. Direct Life Energy to follow your footsteps. Each time your foot touches the ground, Light Energy from both your feet and hands enters into and Blesses Planet Earth.

4. Visualize sending Energy deep into the ground, soothing and clearing Earth Energy as you walk, and nourishing Planet Earth.

5. Say a Blessing while you are walking:

Thank you, Creator, for this Sacred Earth on which I have the privilege of walking right now! Thank you for the abundance that Planet Earth constantly gives, feeding and sustaining us! As I walk today, with each step I passionately and enjoyably send my Blessings that through my Walk, Planet Earth may know the true love, appreciation, and excitement of a Human Angel!

6. Turn around and notice the Trail of Light you are creating behind you...............it looks sparkly, making everything radiate!

This activity builds confidence, grounds you, and sends a Blessing into Planet Earth at the same time!

Strengthening Ceremony

During this Ceremony, you place a series of Energy Balls around your body. This helps you create a thicker, resilient and dependable Overall Energy Body and allows your inner strength to come out of you.

Rinse your hands in water between each Energy Ball, and take your time.

1. Form Energy Ball #1 in the Nurturing position. Appreciate yourself by thinking of a few activities that you enjoy, and bring this vibration into the Energy Ball. Place the Energy Ball above your head, then bring your hands and the Energy Ball slowly downwards to your feet.

2. Form Energy Ball #2 in the Charging position. Look into the Energy Ball and notice how *Life Essence* is moving around[71]. Place this Energy Ball into your solar plexus with a Blessing of Thankfulness for Life! Allow this intensified Life Energy to relax you as it travels through your nervous system, and then exudes from your skin and feeds your Overall Energy Body.

3. Form Energy Ball #3 in the Charging position. Blow a gentle stream of air into the area between your hands with the intention that your Overall Energy Body will be stronger and able to handle any situation that occurs. Place this Energy Ball around you, joining the other layers of your Overall Energy Body.

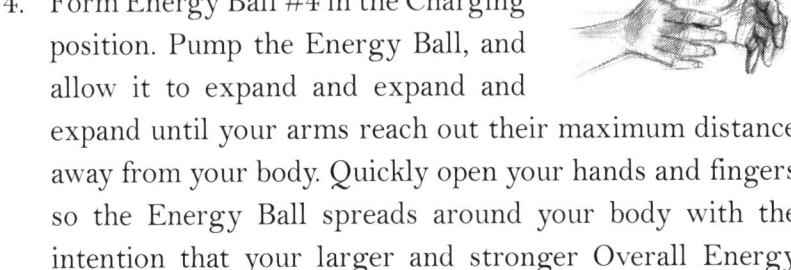

4. Form Energy Ball #4 in the Charging position. Pump the Energy Ball, and allow it to expand and expand and expand until your arms reach out their maximum distance away from your body. Quickly open your hands and fingers so the Energy Ball spreads around your body with the intention that your larger and stronger Overall Energy Body overflows with light and invincibility!

5. Form Energy Ball #5 in the Radiant position at shoulder height. Slowly turn around 360 degrees in a clockwise

---

71 *Go to Seeing the Essence of Life, page 164.*

direction. This creates a circle of Light Energy around you. Notice how it connects to all the layers from the previous Energy Balls. Your Overall Energy Body increases in radiance![72]

 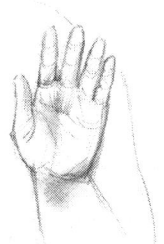

6. Form Energy Ball #6 in the Grounding position. Direct the Energy from your hands deep into Planet Earth, noticing how Earth Energy enters into your body, and providing you with a solid Earth Energy, stabilizing your Overall Energy Body[73].

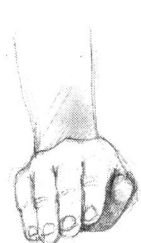 

7. Form Energy Ball #7 in the Light Connection position. Send Energy through your hands high into the atmosphere. Feel that the Energy you receive expands into a Column of Light around you that reaches from the core of Planet Earth, very high into the atmosphere. You are in the middle of it and being charged with very pure, sacred Light. Notice how you are connected to the Sun and the source of Life.

---

72 *See Ceremony to Bless Humanity, page 184.*
73 *See Grounding, page 47.*

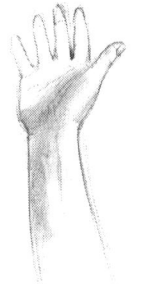 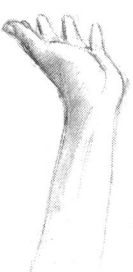

8. Form Energy Ball #8 in the Cleansing position. Acknowledge each layer of Energy that you just placed around you, and notice that they make your Overall Energy Body shine, feel stronger, and more resilient! Place this Energy Ball around your body, feel yourself Blessed and enjoy!

Energy Ball Dance Ceremony

Dancing with the Energy Ball is simple, intuitive, and can be very playful! The intensity of your Life Energy flow increases as you meet your Dancer Within!

1. Prepare a playlist of gentle instrumental music, something that inspires you. Make sure you have ample space in which to move.

2. Form an Energy Ball in the Charging position. Envision yourself Dancing with flowing body movements filled with Light, thereby meeting your Dancer Within.

3. Move the Ball from side to side in time with the music.

4. Hum and sing along with the song, as you Dance. This greatly increases the Energetic flow through your body, and feeds your inner desire to move.

5. Close your eyes, noticing how the Energy Ball connects your Dancer Within to your Overall Energy Body.

6. Pay attention to the emotions that arise during the Dance, acknowledge and honor them.

7. Go into your sensations, feel the Energy moving through your body, and notice how it participates in flowing with the musical vibrations.

8. Bring the Energy Ball around your body by widely expanding your arms, and turn around in a clockwise circle a few times.

Other ideas about Dancing with the Energy Ball

• Play around with the different shapes you can make with the Energy Ball.

• Notice that your Overall Energy Body changes as you expand and contract the Energy Ball in time to the music.

• Allow different parts of your body to lead the movement.

• Play a faster rhythm, increasing the circulation of Life Energy.

• Experiment and explore with the combination of the Energy Ball, music, and moving your body!

• While Dancing, you can guide the Energy Ball into the specific parts of your body to assist in releasing and discharging stuck vibrations.

• When you finish Dancing, move your hands into the Cleansing position and allow the vibrant experience that you just had to integrate into your body.

Meeting the Dancer Within

The Energy Ball guides us into connecting with the part of us that loves to express itself through movement.

When we meet this inner power, we enter into a seemingly endless flow of Life Energy. Our body moves in ways we could never imagine. With each movement, a vibrant surge runs throughout our body systems, stimulating us spiritually, emotionally, consciously, and physically.

A vibrant healing burst of Life Energy is sent out of our body that affects everyone in our vicinity. When two people join together and Dance from the place of the Dancer Within, the experience a magnification of Life Energy!

Follow this activity with the Collective Dancing with the Energy Ball activity[74].

---

74   *See Collective Dancing, page 109.*

Story ~ Peace Pole ~ May Peace Prevail on Earth

During the 1998 Jerusalem Celebration of Light Gathering, my friend, Jimmy Twyman, mailed me a Peace Pole from the World Peace Prayer Society. This symbol of Peace stood two meters high, and was inscribed with the words: "May Peace Prevail on Earth" in 4 languages and alphabets: English, Hebrew, Arabic, and Japanese.

The pole was charged with vibrations of Peace using the Energy Ball for Peace Ceremony, and ceremoniously placed into the ground on Mitzpeh Kerem (Hirbet Hamame) in the Jerusalem Forest.

Inspired by this Peace Ceremony, the World Peace Prayer Society sent me 12 more Peace Poles! With the help of many friends, particularly Hagit Raanan, we ceremoniously planted them in Israel and Palestine. Every one of them has a fascinating story.

It has been estimated that there are over 200,000 Peace poles around the world. You can make or buy a Peace Pole, and charge it by using the Energy Ball for Peace Ceremony![75]

---

75   *See Appendix 1, page 207*

Chapter 18: What you can do!

This chapter invites you to spread the Peaceful Vibrations of the Energy Ball.

- Introduce the Energy Ball to Others
- Building Energy Ball Friendships
- Energy Ball Exploration Teams
- Organize a Collective Energy Ball for Peace Ceremony
- Sunday Middle East Peace Blessing Ceremony

Introduce the Energy Ball to Others

Teaching the Energy Ball to others is easy. Use this or a similar introduction:

I am reading a book about the Energy Ball and its many uses. I have learned to:

- Use it to enhance my Life experiences
- Increase my Energy level and feel more radiant
- Send Blessings for healing, Peace and bringing the Creator's Light into the world
- Experience many sensations with the Energy Ball

Would you like to join me and learn to form an Energy Ball?

Explain to them that the Energy Ball is a way to condense and focus Life Energy, and add in whatever else you feel will encourage them to form an Energy Ball with you.

- Teach them to form the Energy Ball, *reference: page (16)*.
- Form a Couple Energy Ball, *reference: page (77)*.
- Sweeping Body activity, *reference: page (97)*.

- Followed by other Energy Ball activities of your choice.
- If they cannot feel the Energy Ball use the Opening Hands Sensations activity, *reference: page (23)*.

Afterwards, invite them to explore this guidebook with you.

Building Energy Ball Friendships

Friendships are built upon common enriching experiences and the positive feelings that come with them. To have a Friend is precious.

The Energy Ball assists us to develop deeper and more enriching relationships by creating a space to be spiritually held and appreciated.

1. Set up a time to meet in a quiet place. If you are not in the same location, connect via telephone or the internet.

2. Each Friend forms an Energy Ball in the Charging position[76].

3. One person shares something short about what is happening in their life; the other person listens attentively. Then they switch roles. How long each one speaks is decided beforehand.

4. Form a Couple Energy Ball together. If you are not in the same location, visualize that you and your friend are in the same room with your Energy Balls merging together as one. When I do this, it feels like I am right next to them![77]

5. Look into your friend's eyes, allowing your Spiritual Connection to deepen.

---

76   *See Charging Position, Page 27.*
77   *See Couple Energy Ball, page 77*

6. Pay attention to how the Couple Energy Ball affects what you sense in your body, and the quality of Life Energy that you are sending out.

7. Tell your partner how this connection affects your Overall Energy Body.

8. Give your Friend an Energy Ball Hug[78]! From a distance, imagine floating over to visit them and giving them a vibrational hug!

9. Each friend says some closing words, then the Energy Ball is lifted up and released with a Blessing!

Afterwards, set up another time to continue meeting together. When you are consistent, both of your Overall Energy Bodies bond and develop your Friendship Energy into a Peace Team[79]!

Energy Ball Exploration Teams

After experiencing the sacredness of the Energy Ball and having developed Friendships, form an Energy Ball Exploration Team in the form of a study group with experiential exercises.

This is a time to:

• Expand upon the Energy Ball philosophy and way of life.

• Learn and explore with the Energy Ball.

• Listen to the stories of the other participants' Energy Ball experiences.

• Enjoy being together and shining your Light!

Your Exploration Team can choose to bring the Energy Ball for Peace Ceremony into your society. Consider together when and where to create ceremonies, such as in parks, college campuses,

---

78   See Energy Ball Hug, page 98
79   See Peace Team, page 68

community centers, private homes, natural settings........ The ceremonies can be on different holidays and celebrations such as the new or full moon, equinox, solstice, or anytime you wish to gather Peace People together.

Organize a Collective Energy Ball for Peace Ceremony

Bring the Spirit of Peace and excitement into your community with an Energy Ball for Peace Ceremony. Start with a small group. This makes it easier for you to become acquainted with the steps of conducting the Ceremony. It is a very important and fulfilling experience to be the organizer[80]!

1. Read over the Collective section[81], and become familiar with the procedure and the terms.

2. Decide on a theme, such as Blessing the Middle East, World Peace, nurturing hungry children, or healing an individual or a nation.

3. Invite a few friends over to your house or another location, then follow the Peace Ceremony Script[82].

4. Ask those who feel the Energy Ball best if they would like to become your Assistants.

5. Go through the Collective Activities[83] and be perceptive to which of them are appropriate once you complete the initial Ceremony.

6. After you have done a few ceremonies and you feel some confidence, invite everyone you know to join you in sending Peace Blessings to our World!!

---

80 See Organizer, page 70
81 See Collective Section, page 66
82 See Peace Ceremony Script, page 84
83 See Collective Activities, page 94

Sunday Middle East Peace Blessing Ceremony

Every Sunday evening, 21- 21:30 Israel standard time, since the late 1990s, Peace People from around the globe have been sending Blessings of Light and Peace to Jerusalem and the Middle East.

It started after the second intifada to assist in calming the collective fear from acts of terror, and to release the effects caused by these traumas.

Our goal is to Bless humanity, Planet Earth, and to bring Human Angels together as a Team of Peace People, and Brighten up Humanity!

No matter where you are located on the globe, you are welcome to participate in a distance Energy Ball for Peace Ceremony! Thank you for holding a Peaceful vibration!!

Please join our Facebook page[84]:

Story ~ Jeanne White Eagle and John Pehrson

One evening a friend invited me to his home in a suburb of Jerusalem to participate in a Singing Circle and to meet a Native

---

American Elder.

That evening I was realized that I had been **Spontaneously Singing** and for a long time. It felt great to be conscious of what I was doing!

After the Singing Circle while conversing with Jeanne and John, I also realized that our vision of bringing Light and Peace to Planet Earth was the same! We became friends, and began to philosophize about World Peace and humanity awakening from their Spiritual siesta.

I was the Coordinator for the Jerusalem Celebration of Light Gathering at that time, and I immediately invited them to attend the following year.

They accepted, and their presence was magical!! They offered several Singing Circles, workshops, shared their wisdom, and led a Native American Peace Pipe Ceremony. Their substantial Spiritual Light greatly added to the Jerusalem Celebration of Light Gathering and the entire Spiritual Peace movement in Israel!

After the gathering and before they left Israel, I received a call from Jeanne, asking to speak with me about an important matter. Jeanne and John came to my home and offered me the opportunity to be the coordinator of the *For The One Dance*. Even though I had no idea what the *For The One Dance* was or what the role entailed, I accepted.

What a great adventure! I learned that the "For The One Dance" is a Ceremony that uses singing, dancing, fasting, and silence to create an internal atmosphere where a Dancer can cleanse themselves at the deepest levels, physically, emotionally, mentally, and spiritually! I also learned that there is a large crew of people to assist these dancers: Drummers, Chiefs, Moon Mothers, Sun Fathers, Cooks, Dog Soldiers, Fire Keepers, Elders. It took a lot of thoughtful planning and work to organize all this!

Being the Coordinator of the "Dance" for 3 years, part of the crew, and a Dancer for several other years, gave me the opportunity to converse more frequently with Jeanne and John, and a strong bond of friendship developed!

Jeanne and John have been bringing their vision and message of Spiritual Peace to Israel since the year 2000. Now, each year or two, they appear here with a fresh gift for the people of Israel and Palestine! They have conducted many ceremonies, including the Stone People Lodge (Sweat Lodge), Peace Pipe Ceremonies, mystical tours, workshops, and all sorts of Spiritual awakening activities. Many times, during their Concerts and Spontaneous Singing Circles we have shared in an Energy Ball for Peace Ceremony!

Jeanne's latest vision is the creation of the *University and Interstellar Communications Center!*

Their latest books are: "Eyes Open, Looking for the Twelve: Blueprint for a New World" and "Mystical Numerology: The Creative Power of Sounds and Numbers".

Read the book by Monty Jaynes: "Journey for the One", to learn about Jeanne White Eagle and John Pehrson's life.

Their work has brought great Blessing to humanity and the sacred Planet we live on!!!

Appendix 1 ~ References

- Energy Ball For Peace: Facebook page: Middle East Blessing https://www.facebook.com/Energy-Ball-For-Peace-Middle-East-Blessing-226962207442966

- Attunement: https://en.wikipedia.org/wiki/Attunement https://attunement.org

- Somatic Experiencing ®: https://somaticexperiencing.com

- Jeanne White Eagle: http://jeannewhiteeagle.com

- John Pehrson: http://mysticalnumerologyonline.com/

- Eliyahu Holley: https://www.youtube.com/user/ElijahsCodes

- Mitzpeh Kerem (Hirbet Hamame): http://www.kkl-jnf.org/tourism-and-recreation/forests-and-parks/jerusalem-forest.aspx

- Peace Poles: http://www.worldpeace.org/

- All Nations Café: http://allnationscafe.org

- Sulha: http://www.sulha.com

Appendix 2 ~ Energy Ball Information
Individual Benefits of the Energy Ball

- Intensifies self-healing power and builds Spiritual potency.
- Assists in self-regulation of the nervous system.
- Brings awareness to the body's Life Energy circulation.
- Calms down and lightens up emotions.
- Invites internal harmony.
- Aging process is smoother!
- Creates an exciting, fun, inspiring, radiant Life!

Collective Benefits of the Energy Ball

- Genuine way to extend Collective Blessings of Peace!
- Enhances and strengthens a group's Collective Spirit.
- People meet and communicate in a relaxed, calm atmosphere.
- Enlivens the group atmosphere.
- Supports cohesiveness in family, group and business relationships.
- Provides power for a collective project or decision.
- Raises the Collective consciousness.

Regularity with the Energy Ball

This is what to expect from using the Energy Ball on a consistent basis:

- The current of *The Excitement of being actively alive* surges through the body!
- An overall relaxation of the body.
- Mental activity calms down, creating clarity of thought.

- More available Life Energy for daily usage.
- Easier to utilize Spiritual Sight.
- Tension and pain are reduced and become less noticeable.
- Fears calm down in intensity and recede from awareness.

Usage of the Energy Ball

Spiritually:

- Blessing food and water
- Developing and opening Spiritual sight, intuition and Spiritual awareness.
- Enhances sending Blessings.
- Direct connection to Creator and Angels.
- An entry into meditation.

Emotionally and Mentally:

- Melts the unreal and creates the ability to be true to oneself.
- Provides a calming effect during challenging circumstances.
- Enhances the decision-making ability.
- Reduces the after effects of a stressful situation.
- Emotional and mental stabilization.
- Creates an inner state of Peacefulness.

Health:

- Brings relaxation to the nerves and muscles.
- Assists the body to heal quicker from operations and illnesses.
- Guides one into a deep restful, healing sleep.
- Provides a way for practitioners to assist their clients in a more meaningful way.

- Feeds the body with Life Energy.
- Improved communication within the body.

Appendix 3 ~ Comments about the Energy Ball

Some friends who are familiar with the Energy Ball wrote comments:

By Christelle Mie`ville, January 2017

I like to say my daughter came to know Energy Balls when she was in my belly. I created them daily and gave some of them to her.

My baby's energy was participating in the creation of the Energy Balls. I felt her interested and happy, like playing a game with Mommy.

After her birth, as soon as we came home, I chose to create an everyday ritual before sleeping at night. Here it is: I let an Energy Ball be created in between my hands and visualized love, bright Light, support and cleansing energies inside the ball. Then I let the ball merge with my daughter's body, and with my hands I guided the ball into every part of the body. In the meanwhile, I spoke to my baby, telling her she can release what she wants to, and let every cell be filled with Light and love. I sometimes saw her body shaking a bit, like discharging. She often moved and smiled.

Now that she has grown up a bit (9 months), my daughter often joins her hands to mine and makes them move too, according to my feelings, to form a bigger and stronger ball. When I felt that some part of her needed particular attention, I created a Light ball and offered it as special help to that particular part of her, for example, the teeth pushing out.

What a joyful and fun time it is to be with her every night and to clean and recharge together!

By Jonathan Font Moxo

Creating an Energy Ball is a very simple and powerful method. When practiced, it allows the person or people creating it to remember our true being. The Energy Ball connects us to a multi-dimensional perspective, as well as sending a particular wave link for a purpose, such as healing for a place, a group, or a phenomenon.

I personally had very powerful experiences during a Collective Energy Ball for Peace Ceremony, ones that inspired and empowered me. They take place as part of Sacred Musical Singing Circles that I conduct. They have had a profound effect on the people who have attended, and towards where we have directed the Collective Energy Ball.

When Jeff Goldstein comes and leads the creation of a Collective Energy Ball for Peace Ceremony, the singing circle always gets a boost of positive energy!

By Efrat Suraqui, MD

There are many tools to empower healing within, and in a way, there are none. For me the Energy Ball is beyond that. It is not a tool, it is a space. A space of simplicity and love. Practicing the Energy Ball gives me a Peaceful feeling and an ability to be rooted in Nature, and between heaven and Earth. It has become a natural habit, part of my life. Thank you, Jeff, for this wonderful present, a discovery of another layer of life.

By Nicole Béguin

(Please note that Nicole uses the term "Light Balls" instead of Energy Balls.)

I use Light Balls in many different ways:

To Bless the food, I am going to eat so that it will digest and bring all the needed nutrients to my body.

To clean and prepare a room before giving a class. This makes people feel good as soon as they enter the room and enables them to benefit fully from my yoga classes.

To lighten the atmosphere to make it calmer while using public transportation when it is heavy and aggressive. In addition, protect myself from all the pollution coming from the cell phones and laptops that are on.

To clean and thank a place in which I will be in.

As soon as I feel aggressiveness, sadness, and fear, in me and around me, I use Light balls to welcome feeling and then transform the emotion into love, Peace and happiness.

And simply, to bring Light and Love at any moment, anywhere.

To facilitate the connection between Earth and all its inhabitants and Heaven, the Universe, Light people.

By Marsea Spiegel

How often do we get to be playful, imaginative, and have fun while simultaneously creating powerful and positive change in the world around us and beyond? The power of transformation is the very nature of the Energy Ball for Peace Ceremony; a worthwhile and most wonderful exercise!

Creating and sharing an Energy Ball is a simple, fun, and satisfying way to experience the power of connection. It begins in a rather uncomplicated way, going inward, opening one's hearts to the Life Force (flow of love) within, bringing focus to that Energy, and simply holding as the Energy strengthens (gaining strength, in fact, from our undivided attention!) Held in the container of our hands, the Energy is concentrated, gains power, and the ball of Energy forms in its own rich substance.

The momentum builds when we share our Energy Ball with another person in the circle. Since the Energy moving through us is in every moment unique, the blending of two such unique Energy Balls creates something entirely new. We truly are creating (from a place of love, no less!) Our Energy Ball recognizes something larger than itself; shifting and accommodating to find alignment in the new and expanded space. This collaboration happens easily and willingly, life longing for itself, and the Energy Ball strengthens and takes on a richer quality. One doesn't have to believe or not believe that this is taking place. It happens regardless; the nature of Energy is ever moving, seeking likeness and a nurturing field in which to grow.

The strength of the collective Energy Ball, held by all in the circle, practically wills itself out of our hands, filled with Blessing and ready for release beyond the scope of ourselves and into the world, on a mission of its own.

By Dhyan Or from All Nations Café

We had a gathering at the All Nations Café one evening in a field in a border zone between Israel and Palestine where we screened a movie about peace activists. Being located here meant we didn't have electricity, and one of our Palestinian members brought a generator. After a few minutes, we realized the generator wouldn't work, and the movie couldn't be shown.

Jeff suggested we do an Energy Ball together, as we did many times before at our gatherings. While we were growing the ball, and sending peaceful Blessings to all the people of the region, the generator coughed and started working. We all enjoyed the film, but more than that, we felt that our collective Energy, through the Energy Ball Ceremony, actually had something to do with bringing electricity back.

Perhaps it could bring peace back as well.

By Sally Klein-Katz

The Energy Ball Ceremony had deep healing vibrations for me. Most of the vibrations I felt focused on many others; however, I also experienced sensations of healing and release within me. It was powerful for me including: forgiveness, letting go, softness and healing sensations. It was all the more powerful and magnified when we merged our personal Energy Balls with each other in the circle. At moments, it felt limitless. I also sensed a glow emanating filled with energy and love.

By Yoav Peck, Sulha Director

At the Sulha Peace Project we often ask Jeff to open events with his Energy Ball Ceremony. Palestinians and Israelis arrive, many with hesitation and anxiety about meeting with the other side. Jeff brings the group together for the Ceremony, and leads us into the activity. I tend to be skeptical about this sort of thing, yet each time I participate I am amazed to experience the energy of our hands. Within minutes, by the end of the brief Ceremony, inevitably the group is touched and joyous, as the energy of connection flows through the space. Jeff's gentle and buoyant warmth melts people's shyness and resistance, and we are left with a sense of community, ready to engage in the work of peacemaking.

By Lucy Hopes and Evyatar Baumer

We went for a Couple Energy Blending Ceremony with Jeff before we got married. Even though Jeff said our energies were well blended before the ceremony we both felt a stronger Energetic connection afterwards.

We got married abroad and then we planned a wedding celebration near home for friends and family. We knew we wanted a ceremony that was Spiritual but not too 'out there' so it would not scare our guests. We decided on an Energy Ball Wedding Ceremony which Jeff facilitated. The ceremony was a perfect follow-up on the Couple Ceremony and also perfect for 150 wedding guests.

At the Ceremony, Jeff clearly explained to our guests about the energy that we all have in our hands and introduced them to the Energy Ball. He had everyone form an Energy Ball by themselves before merging into twos, fours and bigger groups. Eventually we made one big energy ball circle. Jeff invited us into the middle of the energy ball and instructed everyone to direct their energy towards us with their hands. Then asked everyone to begin moving towards us until our guests were surrounding the two of us saying Blessings and then picking up the ball up and releasing our Wedding Energy Blessings into the sky.

We felt that the ceremony really brought everyone together and made everyone a part of our Wedding Blessing Ceremony. This emphasized the Spiritual aspect of our marriage without a religious context.

Afterwards, many of our guests told us how much they enjoyed the wedding and how unique it was. We think a big part of our guests' enjoyment came from the good vibes we created with the energy ball. Our experience of the Energy Ball was uplifting and happy. The thing we most appreciated about the energy ball on our wedding day was a grounding, peaceful and uplifting energy which was much needed after all the planning.

We practice meditation with the energy ball, always finding it very soothing and relaxing, grounding and uplifting.

By Belle Fine-Cohen, M.S. ~ Writing Assistant's Story

Little did I think that I would be helping to compile the Energy Ball for Peace Ceremony Guide, which in reality is a book that brings Understanding, Peace, Love and Life into the world.

I met Jeff Goldstein at a macrobiotic potluck dinner and lecture. After the lecture, he offered to drive me home and during the ride he told me about his work as a Life Coach, Attunement and Somatic Experiencing Practitioner, Trauma Therapist, and, of course, the Energy Ball.

Being a therapist myself, I was looking for someone to help me get rid of an old trauma of being assaulted that I could not accomplish on my own. Instinctively I knew Jeff was the one that could help me.

The next day I called him to set-up an appointment, and the rest is history.

We became friends and colleagues with a deep understanding of how energy works spiritually, emotionally and physically in the body.

One day at the Spiritual home of our late friend Eliyahu Holley, he told us about the book he was writing on the Energy Ball and that he was looking for someone to read it to and, of course, I volunteered, and that is how I became the editor of this book, and learned all about the Energy Ball and more. I found that it complemented and enhanced what I was doing in my personal life and private practice.

The opportunity to compile the material for this book gave me the opportunity to see Jeff, in his humanness and how he sets an example of someone who truly practices what he preaches while walking his talk! He is truly a very mystical being.

Many thanks to HaShem (God) for bringing Jeff into my life and opening the door to a better knowledge of myself, my Nefesh (soul), and the world we live in and becoming a more attuned *helper* on the road to Peace, Understanding and Enlightenment in the world.

JEFFREY GOLDSTEIN

Alternative Trauma Therapist

Somatic Experiencing® Practitioner

Attunement Instructor & Therapist

Spiritual Guidance

Resides in Jerusalem, Israel

Jeffrey Goldstein grew up in Massapequa, New York. Early

in life he learned that there is a *city consciousness* and a natural consciousness. His choice of following the natural way, in the midst of the suburbs, led him into learning philosophy, carpentry, and how to help people heal themselves from life's traumas.

Jeffrey says: "As soon as I heard about 'war', I became passionate about Peace, and have been stimulating both inner and outer Peace ever since. I walk in a natural setting every day, communicating with the elements and stimulating my natural part."

He lives in a small neighborhood on the west side of Jerusalem called Yefe Nof, (beautiful view). On one side is the natural Judean Hills, and on the other side the bustling city of Jerusalem.

Jeffrey is married to Leah and they have two daughters, Lilach and Shira, who are passionate about life!

His private practice takes him around Israel, Palestine, Switzerland and the USA, and he enjoys being a Mystical Guide around Jerusalem and Israel.

For more information about location of upcoming Energy Ball for Peace Ceremonies, private ceremonies, lessons, and instructor classes: www.jeffgoldsteinattuner.com

Printed in Great Britain
by Amazon